The Michelangelo Principle

The Michelangelo Principle

*How Busy Leaders Accomplish
More by Doing Less*

Paul Rulkens

BEP

BUSINESS EXPERT PRESS

Leader in applied, concise business books

The Michelangelo Principle:
How Busy Leaders Accomplish More by Doing Less

Copyright © Business Expert Press, LLC, 2025.

First manuscript edit by Nancy Jergins

Illustrations by Dennis Luijer: prismatica.nl

Book Cover Design by Saga 99D

Interior design by S4Carlisle Publishing Services, Chennai, India

First published in 2025 by
Business Expert Press, LLC
222 East 46th Street, New York, NY 10017
www.businessexpertpress.com

ISBN-13: 978-1-63742-846-7 (paperback)
ISBN-13: 978-1-63742-847-4 (e-book)

Business Expert Press Human Resource Management and Organizational
Behavior Collection

First edition: 2025

10 9 8 7 6 5 4 3 2 1

EU SAFETY REPRESENTATIVE
Mare Nostrum Group B.V.
Mauritskade 21D
1091 GC Amsterdam
The Netherlands
gpsr@mare-nostrum.co.uk

Description

Achieve More by Doing Less

Success in leadership often becomes its own trap. The better you perform, the more complexity, noise, and demands pile onto your plate. But what if the key to extraordinary results isn't doing more, but removing what doesn't matter?

The Michelangelo Principle: How Busy Leaders Accomplish More by Doing Less challenges you to rethink leadership. Like Michelangelo carving *David*, true mastery lies not in adding, but in chiseling away the unnecessary to reveal your full potential.

This book is designed for **Corporate Olympians**—high-performing leaders caught in the paradox of success. With fresh perspectives, innovative concepts, and actionable tools, you'll learn to sidestep inefficiencies, eliminate distractions, and amplify your leadership impact.

- **Break Free from Leadership Traps**—Avoid time-wasters, zombie projects, and the illusion of competence.
- **Build Resilience**—Shift from rigidity to adaptability with systems that thrive in uncertainty.
- **Activate Your Team**—Transform committees into high-performance teams that own results.
- **Leave a Legacy**—Stop leaving trails of activity and start building systems that outlast you.

From **The Valley of Death** to **The Two Buckets Problem**, *The Michelangelo Principle* introduces powerful frameworks and practical tools inspired by disciplines as diverse as physics, history, and engineering. It challenges conventional wisdom and offers practical steps to streamline your leadership, sharpen decision making, and focus on what matters most.

This is not just another book on productivity. It's a roadmap for creating a simpler, stronger, and more impactful path to leadership success.

Paul Rulkens is a global expert in high-performance leadership. He has helped Fortune 500 companies, including McKinsey, Siemens, Nestlé, Mercedes-Benz, and Uber, achieve breakthrough results by doing less.

A sought-after speaker, his TED talk *Why the Majority Is Always Wrong* has garnered over 6 million views. As a senior fellow at The Conference Board, Paul equips executives with proven strategies to accelerate growth and build high-performance organizations.

Contents

List of Figures

Introduction

This book is designed to help you accomplish more by doing less, and in keeping with this promise, I will keep this introduction concise.

Imagine you are a Corporate Olympian: a professional who has dedicated years of effort and focus to mastering your chosen field. Your leadership has been shaped by discipline, resilience, and an ability to adapt under pressure. But what happens when every new success leads to greater complexity, more demands, and an ever-expanding workload? The better you perform, the more weight is added to your shoulders—a cycle that feels both inevitable and exhausting.

The premise of this book is simple: Advancing to the next level of leadership is not about increasing your effort or raising your standards of Olympian excellence. It's about stepping back, looking at the bigger picture, and ruthlessly removing what is unnecessary, ineffective, and erroneous. Like Michelangelo chiseling away everything that wasn't David, your next breakthrough will come not from adding but from subtracting.

This book is divided into two parts:

Part 1: Thinking Differently

This section introduces a set of fresh perspectives designed to challenge conventional thinking and common leadership traps. Drawing inspiration from disciplines as diverse as physics, history, and engineering, you will learn how to avoid the illusion of control, embrace optionality, and replace complexity with clarity.

Part 2: Acting Differently

Here, you will find a practical toolkit comprising 25 techniques that bring the insights from the first part into action. These tools are designed to simplify, streamline, and amplify your leadership effectiveness, enabling you to lead with precision and purpose.

Information is abundant, but action is scarce. If you're willing to let go of what no longer serves you, this book will guide you to a simpler, sharper, and more impactful way of leading.

Let's begin.

PART 1

Thinking Differently

CHAPTER 1

The Michelangelo Principle

My Nemesis Subject

Most of us have a nemesis subject: a part of our learning journey that we cannot easily grasp, either because our brains are not wired for the subject, or it simply bores us.

My nemesis subject was organic chemistry, and it included a 600-page textbook that I needed to learn by heart. It sounded like a lot of work to me. I was 21 years old and organic chemistry was boring me to death. Yet, as a diligent student, mastering organic chemistry was essential if I wanted to earn my coveted master's degree in chemical engineering.

What to do?

My solution was not overly elegant, but it was rather effective. First, it involved skipping all of the left pages of the organic chemistry textbook—I figured that anything important would be repeated on the right page. Second, I had learned from experience that mastering a subject and acing an exam about that subject were two very different things. Since organic chemistry professors are very busy people, they tend to recycle exam questions. The number of organic molecules is infinite; the number of exam questions about organic molecules is not.

I used these two insights to play the system, and I passed the dreaded exam. In hindsight, the amount of time I had to spend to get an acceptable grade was ridiculously low.

This was not my first attempt to get the maximum result with the least amount of effort, but it was the first time I allowed myself to think about it strategically. Up until then, my shortcuts typically resulted in sloppy work that needed to be fixed soon after. This strategic shortcut, however, showed much more promise.

Organic chemistry became the catalyst for my obsession with strategic high performance. I define this as the ability to consistently achieve big goals in the laziest way possible. Consistency is important because any desired result must be repeatable to climb the ladder of great achievement. A one-hit wonder lacks the foundation on which a bright future can be built.

Big goals are important because thinking small is already done in abundance. If you buy and open an average popular magazine at the airport, it's full of ideas and insights which only marginally improve the condition of mankind. Yet they are hyped as the pinnacle of innovation.

And finally, a lazy outlook is a healthy approach to life. This does not imply that you, the reader, are lazy. I assume that by picking up this book you may be one of the most curious and hardest-working people on the planet. However, if you can go from A to B in the laziest way possible, you will have the time, energy, and resources to do other things as well, like reading this book, starting a company, or traveling to Mars.

Being lazy in the context of high performance is a good thing in our modern times.

Understanding Our Current Reality

Let's consider our reality first. We compete in a global marketplace where smart and ambitious people enter the workforce nonstop. This means that we can no longer rely on brute force, exemplary character, and hard work to carve out our niche—the place where we can dominate and ignore the external world. Or as business gurus would tell us, we need to work smarter.

This has always puzzled me: What does it even mean to work smarter?

For a lean sigma expert, it means improving efficiency by looking at optimizing processes and systems. Thus, we end up with a large flock of very smart and busy people who aim to squeeze the last drop out of any operation.

For a content marketer, it means outsourcing as much as possible to artificial intelligence (AI). In this case, we find ourselves building a new dystopian playing field where content-creating AI is competing for the eyeballs of content-absorbing AI.

For an aerospace engineer, it implies using more advanced computational models and systems to create the airplane of the future.

In all cases, it's about more–better–faster. The core idea is that progress enables us to create more, create better, and create faster. This is fueled by our human nature to find and break through barriers.

In the Roman era, the travel speed barrier was determined by the stamina of a horse. Modern technology changed all of this. For all practical purposes, our current travel speed barrier is determined by how fast a commercial airplane can fly. No doubt, in the future, this barrier will be broken again by new technology. Perhaps the Star Trek Transporter is closer than we think.

We also need to realize that more–better–faster is a relative concept. If an aerospace engineer can design a new plane in substantially less time, her colleague working diligently for the competition on the other side of the world will be able to do this, too. The perceived advantage melts away over time. With greater global connection, any competitive advantage disappears faster than free beer at Mardi Gras.

This is the Red Queen Conundrum. In Lewis Carroll's *Alice's Adventures in Wonderland*, the Red Queen noted that you need to run as fast as you can simply to remain in the same spot. If you want to go somewhere else, you need to run faster. This is how modern work often feels: The reward for solving complex problems is the opportunity to solve even more complex problems. The better you get, the better you better get.

Embracing the mindset of more–better–faster is therefore only a temporary relief for a fundamentally modern problem. Being ahead is always relative to the competition, and the competition tends to catch up faster every day.

This explains why modern corporations spend more and more resources on lobbying and influencing legislation. The return on investment of these activities is often much bigger than that of innovation. Many of our current laws are explicitly designed to carve out a profitable niche and keep out competition. Take, for example, REACH: a set of laws to govern the safe introduction of new chemicals in Europe. The intent was to increase the safety of EU citizens. The result, however, is that small competitors don't have the financial means to meet REACH requirements, only the big players do.

If we want to consistently achieve big goals with the least amount of effort, the more–better–faster approach is becoming harder every day.

It's time to rethink our approach to high performance.

The Conspiracy Against Thinking

When was the last time you spent a full hour thinking with only pen and paper? It's one of the favorite questions I ask my executive clients. These are some of the answers I've received:

> *Thinking? I haven't used pen and paper in years.*
> *Come to think of it, I only take the time to think while taking my morning shower.*
> *Frankly, I have no time to think. My schedule is packed wall to wall.*
> *I think once a year: During the Christmas break, I make a plan. The rest of the year, I simply execute.*
> *When I walk the dog, it's also thinking time.*

These are shocking acknowledgments. An executive is paid for judgment. Judgment requires deep thinking. Deep thinking requires thinking time. It's clear that our priorities are wrong.

This lack of deep thinking is not limited to executives. It has penetrated all levels of our society. Modern technology only accelerates this trend.

Take AI. With the advent of AI, humanity has reached two peaks.

The first peak is the perfection of systems to access complete and accurate knowledge. This process started more than 5,000 years ago in ancient Sumer, with clay tablets recording the first business transactions. That innovation led to advanced storage of information; from books to libraries, and from the Internet to the Cloud. It heralded a shift from information access to information use.

The advent of AI has also birthed the second peak: More advanced systems to access and interpret information have led to more decision making being outsourced. Think of Enterprise Resource Systems such as SAP, or stock trading algorithms widely used on Wall Street.

Wouldn't it be great if we used the newly available thinking-energy to think about even more useful stuff? Alas, the opposite is often true. As an example, the availability of more business data has led to more key performance indicators (KPIs) and more meetings about KPIs.

Since it seems that every single new innovation is now aimed at reducing human thinking, I call this the conspiracy against thinking. Instead of using our brains to engage in deep thinking, we are creating an environment to further shield it from dealing with uncertainty, ambiguity, and complexity. Smart systems now either tell us what to do, or simply decide to do it for us.

The risk is that we slowly unlearn how to think. This, of course, makes us vulnerable and unable to deal with the next crisis.

It compromises our achievement.

But what is achievement?

Thinking About Achievement

The formula for achievement is simple:

$$\text{Achievement} = \text{skill} + \text{luck}$$

Skill contains three components: expertise, talent, and character.

Expertise is the result of experience and learning. Typically, time and training build expertise. A master chef develops her expertise by doing a lot of cooking for a lot of people for a long time.

Talent is our natural propensity to learn a skill, and sets the ceiling of our performance. I could spend a lifetime learning how to cook, but my cooking ability will always be constrained by the fixed limits of my inferior taste buds. On a similar note, my average height will always prevent me from becoming a high-earning basketball player.

Finally, character is our persistence to learn and persevere, especially when times are tough. The brilliant prodigy who gives up at the first sign of trouble will never obtain significant skills.

Understanding these components has implications for building skills, maximizing talent, and developing character.

A systematic approach to accelerated learning will rapidly improve your expertise, and therefore your skill. This requires the absorption of new knowledge.

Statistics show that the amount of scientific data doubles every 2 years. At the same time, the impact of individual scientific articles is diminishing. This means that our ability to distinguish noise from signal becomes more important, and simultaneously more difficult.

With this in mind, how can you effectively gain useful knowledge? For example, if you want to build a high-performance team, where do you start?

The first level is to access quick and readily available information. I call this shallow knowledge. Think of a YouTube video that explains in 5 minutes how to build a success environment for your team. You get immediate insights, but the insights may not be very deep, or even accurate.

The second level is reading books written by experts on the subject. This is deep knowledge: You absorb the condensed wisdom of many years of experience. This, however, takes time, and much of the information may not be relevant for the current issues you're facing.

The third level is private access to personal knowledge; an expert masterclass combines condensed insights with an opportunity to discuss the practical applications of your specific issues.

The guiding principle of gaining knowledge to rapidly build skills is that you need to go to the next level when reaching a knowledge plateau. Watching more YouTube videos will not replace the knowledge you can gain from reading books, and expanding your reading list will not substitute for personal access to content experts.

If you want to have more expertise, decide first which knowledge level you actually require. Then, implement a strategy to get there with the least amount of effort.

The most important aspect of talent is that it's overrated when you want to become good at something. The reason is that talent only becomes relevant when expertise is honed to a very high level. The difference between two effective marketing executives is more often than not determined simply by the length of their experience. Talent only becomes important at the highest levels of performance.

Finally, character is destiny. Persistence, ownership, and proactivity determine the speed at which expertise is built, and talent is revealed.

In its simplest form, the recipe for building skill is to choose an area where you have a natural talent which makes it easy for you to learn, while raising the bar for new behavioral standards which will maintain momentum when times are tough.

You also need to be lucky.

The Role of Luck

What's luck? When thinking about luck, what immediately comes to mind are casinos, lotteries, or the inheritance of a faraway, rich relative. Luck paints a picture of known probabilities to win or lose something. It can be either good luck (fortune) or bad luck (unfortunate).

Luck plays a major part in our life.

The chance meeting that propelled your career.

The freak traffic accident that put you out of action for a long time.

The book you read that inspired you with a great idea.

Can luck be controlled? It's true that the harder you work, the luckier you get. For example, if you continue to test new ideas, it doesn't impact the probability of success of each idea. It does, however, impact the probability of success of your entire idea portfolio.

We can certainly influence luck, yet we can't guarantee results.

To improve our results as a business executive, we need to understand the game we play.

The Game We Play

Since our achievement is based on a combination of luck and skill, let's review the implications of some real-life scenarios.

Think of a lottery winner. Since playing the lottery is purely a game of chance, the luck component of the achievement of the lottery winner is 100 percent.

An effective test to see if any skill is involved, is to ask if it's possible to buy a lottery ticket that is a guaranteed loser. Since this is not possible—you cannot deliberately play to lose by joining a lottery—its outcome is purely based on luck.

Now, think of the world champion of chess. Since chess is a completely transparent game with defined and unchanging rules, the skill part of the achievement is very high, but it's not 100 percent. After all, an annoying mosquito may ruin a good night's sleep just before a very important game.

So, are we really in control?

The Illusion of Control

When I was very small, my father installed a toy steering wheel that was fixed to the backseat of our car. In this way, I could not only mimic his steering wheel movements but also control the car myself. This was fun until it dawned on me that my steering wheel only worked when I copied the precise movements of my father. When I rebelled and did the opposite, the car somehow only listened to my dad. This was my first encounter with the illusion of control.

Trying to control your destiny by frantically turning a fake steering wheel is a very typical human behavior. Our mind automatically tries to explain current results by making a connection with our past actions. Two random points on a graph automatically turn into a line. The concept of cause and effect is deeply ingrained in our thinking.

In his famous experiment, Pavlov was able to condition chickens to connect certain behaviors to obtaining food. The food distribution, however, was random, yet the chickens continued to exhibit the behaviors which they thought would trigger the appearance of food. It was the ultimate example of the Illusion of Control.

We are not much different from chickens after all.

Our mind is an explanation machine; it tries to make sense of the world around us. It has the habit of explaining that good results are due to our own skill, and bad results are due to encountering bad fortune.

Think of the business executive who proudly explains that the massive growth was caused by a combination of the right strategy, the right people, and the right leadership. A year later, the same executive solemnly declares that the disappointing growth was caused by volatile exchange rates, a global pandemic, and economic headwinds. Suddenly, the right strategy, the right people, and the right leadership have taken a backseat.

To maintain our sanity, we delude ourselves by thinking we have much more control over our results than we actually have.

Taking back real control means that we first need to get clarity in our thinking.

Clarity in Thinking

What makes us uniquely human is our ability to think about thinking.

So, what's the purpose of thinking?

If you ask this question to a philosopher, he will have a thousand different answers. We think to survive, we think because we are, we think to improve, we think to find meaning, and so forth. However, if you ask this question to a brain scientist, she will only have one answer: The purpose of thinking is to stop thinking.

Thinking is a high-energy-consuming activity. Thus, whenever we think, we think as short and efficiently as possible. After that, we quickly return to autopilot.

Autopilot is a state of mind where we subconsciously engage with the outside world. We rely on routines such as brushing our teeth, walking the dog, or watching videos. Sometimes, however, we are able to elevate our conscience to break through the autopilot. We may have encountered this ourselves when driving a car. Turning into the driveway to our house, we suddenly ask ourselves what we've been doing the past 10 minutes.

Some estimates tell us that we run on autopilot more than 95 percent of our lives. The conscious state is rare, and it means that the vast amount of our behavior is driven by habits, routines, and heuristics.

Standard habits, routines, and heuristics work well in a controlled, certain, and organized world. Our world, however, is uncontrolled, uncertain, and chaotic. Effective habits, routines, and heuristics may not be effective in all circumstances. When we apply them in circumstances that require a different approach, we get stuck.

To get unstuck, our first priority is to understand when we need to step out of our habits, routines, and heuristics, and really think. This requires that we become aware of some of the thinking biases we habitually employ.

The Turkey Problem

The turkey is absolutely convinced that the butcher loves it. It is being fed, housed, and taken care of for about 20 months. Then Thanksgiving arrives, and the world of the turkey changes dramatically in an instant. Nassim Taleb calls this the Turkey Problem. The life of the turkey tells us that it's very dangerous to extrapolate the past to predict the future. Yet it's a very common approach in our professional world. For example, we all know the typical sophisticated process for the new annual department budget: Let's use our existing budget and add a certain percentage on top of it. That's not the only issue, though. The life of the turkey has another, even more disturbing implication: Ruin occurs for the turkey at the very moment it has the maximum amount of solid data that everything is fine! The day before Thanksgiving, it has 20 months of real data which tells it that all is well. Unbeknownst to the turkey, it's also its last day on this planet.

If you want to make your team and your organization more robust, resilient, and ready to deal with the next crisis, you need to ask a deeply uncomfortable and almost paranoid question: Where are we running on autopilot in our organization and, where is all well? It's precisely there that you have the biggest risk of becoming a turkey.

Cargo Cult Thinking

Cargo cult thinking is the belief that if we simply emulate the visible effects of achievement, real achievement will follow automatically. Especially when the initial results look promising, we tend to think we are skilled, while in reality, we are lucky. The term cargo cult was first coined after World War II. During the conflict, several remote-island-based airfields were established in the Pacific for military purposes, baffling the indigenous populations. Often, limited or no contact was established between the islanders and the more modern military forces. When the military finally left the islands, the original inhabitants tried to recreate the airfields using bamboo, stone, and other available materials, waiting for the planes to return. Hence the name cargo cult thinking: If you build it, they will come.

Cargo cult thinking is not limited to those unfamiliar with cause and effect; it has a prominent place in modern business thinking, as well. For instance, Elizabeth Holmes, the notorious CEO of Theranos, started wearing a black turtleneck to mimic Steve Jobs in order to practice reality distortion of her own. She was initially very successful. But, as the downfall of Theranos has shown, what she actually did was mix up cause and effect: The rooster that crows in the morning doesn't cause the sun to rise. Likewise, cajoling the rooster to crow earlier will not make a longer day.

The Silent Graveyard

During World War II, a group of statisticians was asked to find ways to reduce the number of Allied airplanes that didn't return from missions in Europe. After studying bullet-hole patterns in aircraft that returned from their missions, the statisticians proposed adding more armor to the areas of the planes where they had been hit the most—wings, tail, and fuselage—but, oddly enough, not on the engines, which had the smallest number of bullet holes per surface area. Then, one statistician asked an interesting question: Where are the missing bullet holes—the ones that would be all over the engine if bullets were equally distributed? The answer was obvious: The missing bullet holes were on the planes that had been shot down and hadn't returned. The critical part of a plane was not where most of the bullet holes were on the returning planes. It was where the bullet holes were on the planes that did not return—the engines, the cockpit, and the fuel system. What we see is all there is. As a result, we ignore a large history of failures in order to predict success.

Mental Substitution

A few years ago, I was in charge of recommending the location for a large production facility to a CEO. The company already owned a smaller production facility. While reviewing the different alternatives, something interesting happened. When I asked several stakeholders, "Which location would be best for the business?" many argued for the existing location. Upon further discussion, it became clear they were convinced that expanding the existing facility would result in the least amount of hassle. They didn't answer the original question, "Which location would be best for the business?" Instead, they answered a different, easier question, "Which location decision would be easiest to execute?"

Replacing a difficult question with an easier one is called mental substitution. For example, the question, "How happy are you with the performance of an individual?" is often replaced with another easier question, "How much do you like the individual?" Mental substitution is a very common mistake. The antidote is a simple follow-up question. "Why, exactly?"

Outsourced Thinking

Recently, I stumbled upon a terrifying story: A hiker got lost in the woods. After several weeks, she was finally found with a lot of difficulty because she had not left any traces behind, such as campfires or shelter. She clearly adhered to the standard rule of hiking in nature: Never disturb the environment. This sensible and practical behavior is great under normal circumstances, but it's disastrous if you're looking to be rescued. This is an example of outsourced thinking: the inability to change course when circumstances change.

It's usually a crisis that unmasks tunnel vision in organizations. For example, a focus on favorable payment terms is a good business practice. Yet there are numerous businesses that have seriously damaged their reputation by not being flexible with their payment terms for their suppliers in these testing times. A blind adherence to rules creates a fossilized organization. Never outsource your thinking to industry-best practices.

Dunning–Kruger Effect

The Dunning–Kruger effect is "a cognitive bias in which unskilled individuals suffer from illusory superiority, mistakenly rating their ability much higher than average. This bias is attributed to a metacognitive inability of the unskilled to recognize their mistakes." This means that if we are completely ignorant and unskilled in a certain area, we often overestimate how well we will perform in that area. An example is cutting vegetables. If you watch a master chef on television chopping carrots, it looks easy. Only when they tell you that it requires a full year of master chef training to learn how to properly cut vegetables do you start to realize there is much more to it than meets the eye. This is the Dunning–Kruger effect in action. Needless to say, the Dunning–Kruger effect can wreak havoc on your best-laid plans.

The Lazy High-Performance Game

If we want to take back control in turbulent times, it's important to become aware of our thinking fallacies. The key idea is to overcome these fallacies so we can focus on playing a game where the impact of our skill is maximized, while the impact of luck is minimized. I call this a lazy high-performance game.

Characteristics of a lazy high-performance game are:

- You can take deliberate actions to lose.
- The rules of the game are clear, transparent, and unchanging.
- There is no path dependency. Imagine thousands of identical worlds. The starting points are identical, yet history repeats itself with some slight changes due to random events. In many of these worlds, the world champion of chess will be the same individual. However, in only one of these worlds, the lottery winner will be the lucky individual. In skill-based games, your achievement is much less path dependent. In a luck-based game, it's purely path dependent.
- With focused practice, you can improve and positively influence your achievement by objective and measurable standards.
- There is a body of work that helps you to improve. The library is stacked with books about chess. It does not contain any reliable books about how to become the next lottery winner.

With this in mind, let's take a closer look at the following examples of games we can play:

- Start-up founder versus start-up investor.
- Astronaut versus NASA engineer.
- Writer of a best-selling book versus book publisher.
- Hedge fund owner versus registered accountant.
- Nobel Prize winner in chemistry versus C-suite executive.

In each of these examples, the skill level on the left is very high. Yet the end result of this high skill level is mainly determined by luck. Only a fraction of all financial experts will become hedge fund managers. Only a few start-ups will make it after the first 5 years. Only a small percentage of all potential astronauts will ever reach space. Only a few excellent writers will turn their talents into best-selling books. Only a few scientists will ever be rewarded with a Nobel Prize.

The painful conclusion is that much of what we call skill-based achievement is less about skill and more about the lucky circumstances where these skills can flourish.

Developing skills is therefore not enough for great achievement. We must choose a game where we can eliminate the luck factor as much as possible.

What does this mean for corporate leaders?

The Michelangelo Principle

After creating the statue of David, the great Italian Renaissance artist Michelangelo was asked how he had accomplished this masterpiece. Michelangelo answered that he looked at the original block of uncut marble, imagined David hidden in there, and simply removed everything that wasn't David.

This powerful insight can be applied to quickly and systematically improve our personal and professional lives.

If we want to play a game where the impact of our skills is maximized, while at the same time the impact of luck is minimized, take out everything that makes you vulnerable to changing circumstances and volatility.

If you want to improve your health, don't set a goal to run a marathon. Start by eliminating alcohol, smoking, and sugar first.

If you want to improve your productivity, don't build the habit of waking up at 5 a.m. Start by cutting down on social media consumption first.

If you want to improve your financial situation, don't try to pick winning stocks. Pay off debt as fast as possible first.

Taking out everything that makes you vulnerable is the superior approach to improvement.

Some time ago, my wife and I had lunch at one of our favorite restaurants. We discussed what sets our preferred establishments apart from others. My wife noticed something interesting: The best places all have a limited menu, with popular dishes done consistently well.

If you want to improve your restaurant business, the ideal approach is actually counterintuitive: Don't try to expand and create new dishes, but simplify and focus on the few dishes you do very well.

Improving your business, organizational, or professional results by removing activities that are not your David is a highly effective and superior approach. It offers three unique advantages when compared to adding new activities.

1. **It reduces volatility.** When significant changes in your environment happen, the probability of bad outcomes becomes less likely. For example, when an economic recession occurs, a simple and trusted meal with consistent high quality will continue to be in high demand.
2. **It creates new opportunities.** A limited, high-quality menu reduces preparation complexity and increases the speed of service and consistency. This, in turn, will boost turnover, growth, and margin.
3. **It's much easier.** Getting rid of ballast on your menu takes much less effort than the complete redesign needed to add new dishes, such as revamping kitchen facilities, teaching new cooking skills, and setting up new suppliers.

The next time you want to start something new, combat the urge and focus on getting rid of deadweight first.

The Michelangelo Principle is therefore the foundation to achieve more with less. It allows you to shift from trying to control the future to building an organization that is ready for anything the future can throw at you.

In the following chapters, we will explore how busy executives can use this principle to massively improve the performance of themselves, their team, and their organization.

Key Actionable Takeaways

1. **Eliminate Unnecessary Tasks**: Review your to-do list and remove tasks that do not directly contribute to your goals. Busywork and nonessential activities drain time and energy that could be better spent on impactful efforts.

2. **Stop Relying on "More–Better–Faster" Strategies**: Abandon the mindset of constantly doing more or working faster to stay ahead. This approach often leads to diminishing returns and burnout. Instead, focus on eliminating inefficiencies and creating sustainable advantages.

3. **Remove Distractions That Undermine Deep Thinking**: Avoid filling your schedule wall to wall or constantly multitasking. Clear time for focused, uninterrupted thought, and minimize reliance on technology that reduces critical thinking.

4. **Cut Out Nonstrategic Goals**: Do not pursue goals simply because they seem achievable or popular. Eliminate objectives that lack alignment with your long-term vision to avoid diluting your focus and resources.

5. **Stop Relying on Past Successes**: Question processes or strategies that worked in the past but may not serve your current reality. Avoid the Turkey Problem by identifying areas where complacency or outdated habits make your organization vulnerable.

6. **Avoid Cargo Cult Thinking**: Do not mimic what others do without understanding the underlying principles. Remove practices that focus on replicating visible success rather than addressing root causes or unique challenges.

7. **Eliminate Excessive Metrics and Meetings**: Stop overloading your team with unnecessary KPIs or endless meetings. Reduce the noise to focus on a few key metrics and discussions that truly drive performance.

8. **Cut Down on Overcomplex Systems**: Simplify processes and systems that have become overly complicated. Streamline operations to reduce friction, improve efficiency, and prepare your organization for unforeseen challenges.

9. **Stop Trying to Control Everything**: Let go of the illusion that you can predict or dictate every outcome. Instead, eliminate rigid practices and focus on adaptability, building a system that thrives in uncertainty.

10. **Remove Activities That Aren't Your "David"**: Audit your personal and organizational efforts to identify what adds little value. Like Michelangelo, carve away the unnecessary to reveal the masterpiece within your core strengths.

CHAPTER 2

Strategic Clarity

Looking for the Next Iceberg

A crisis is a powerful way to focus the mind. When the *Titanic* hit an iceberg, clear-headed people acted quickly to make the best of a bad situation. There was no confusion about priorities, despite the urban legend of the band playing on until the end. A crisis brings simplicity out of complexity, clarity out of confusion, and decisiveness out of hesitation. No wonder this sense of laser-like focus is addictive for many executives and organizations.

However, too many organizations subconsciously create serial urgencies to get things done because this approach does have its advantages. First, the organization automatically moves in the right direction. Second, the leaders who solve the current crisis are viewed as heroes. But there are downsides.

These Titanic organizations share several negative characteristics:

- Leaders are valued and promoted based on their problem-solving abilities, not their problem-prevention skills.
- Meetings and conversations primarily focus on issues, not opportunities.
- Little meaningful and strategic progress is made between crises.
- There are limited systems and processes for crisis prevention and anticipation.
- Small issues are ignored, quickly turning into major problems.
- There is high talent attrition.
- Action is valued far more than deep thinking.

Subconsciously, risky decisions are made to ensure that a new iceberg is always on the horizon. One IT organization I worked with intentionally set unrealistic business goals at the beginning of each year to guarantee frantic activity by year's-end. The thinking was that these overly ambitious goals would inspire employees to go the extra mile. Instead, they led to the loss of good employees who were tired of playing this predictable yet exhausting game.

This is a powerful lesson for busy leaders: Strategic clarity for yourself and your organization will massively boost performance. Eliminating the urge to look for a new iceberg is a good first step. Let's explore what else needs to be done.

Strategic Thinking Is Sequential

Imagine an organization facing turbulent times. The management team convenes in an emergency meeting, and the CEO desperately asks for good ideas. The assumption is that creativity only occurs in this classic corporate ritual—the team meeting. Naturally, the responses are less than inspiring, so the CEO concludes that the organizational structure does not support creative thinking. Human resources propose a new structure. The immediate result is mass confusion: Who reports to whom, and what are the new roles and responsibilities?

This does not help the organization navigate turbulent times. As urgency increases, it's necessary to shift gears. The focus moves to action. "Do something, don't just stand there." Busyness becomes predominant, yet the resulting chaos produces little real progress.

At this point, it becomes clear that collaboration is missing, and the organization is not aligned in its approach and behaviors. A company-wide program is initiated to build high-performance, collaborative teams. Off-site, the teams build rafts, cook together, and construct towers from marshmallows and spaghetti. They get to know each other well, yet none of the spaghetti towers lead to improved results.

Next, the CEO turns to external consultants. They observe the chaos and begin with a profound question: "What does a successful future look like?" With this, the organization finally initiates strategic thinking.

This pattern is, unfortunately, very common in many organizations. It's caused by the fact that strategic clarity is both consequential and sequential:

- Understand what the vision of massive success looks like.
- Define the behavioral standards necessary to achieve the vision.

- Engage the organization and brainstorm creative solutions.
- Organize and structure all ideas and resources in a strategic plan.
- Take significant action.

Busy leaders sometimes skip steps or execute them in the wrong order such as: brainstorm, organize, execute, establish behavioral standards, and formulate a vision.

Let's take a closer look at the typical mistakes to avoid in each of the four stages prior to taking significant action.

The Trap of a Utopian Vision

A vision is an imaginative and inspiring view of a magnificent future. Without vision, there are no goals. Without goals, there is no direction— any performance or creativity is based on luck, not skill. There are many ways to develop a vision. My favorite is to ask, "What would we do if we knew we couldn't fail?"

However, something worse than having no vision is having a radical, utopian vision that has these characteristics:

- Requires massive sacrifices from others. ("They have to ...")
- Is based on a romantic and unrealistic concept of the past. ("Return to ...")
- Opposes basic human nature. ("People must be forced to ...")
- Relies on magical technological developments. ("As soon as ...")
- Is grounded in apocalyptic thinking. ("If we don't, then ...")
- Is rigid and uncompromising in its ultimate goal. ("There is no alternative but ...")
- Attracts zealots. ("Only those who ...")
- Most importantly, it lacks joy, fun, and optimism ("Only after ...").

If your strategy or vision includes one or more of these characteristics— whether explicitly stated or implied—it's time to step back and rethink your approach to future success.

Additionally, a vision is meaningless if it can't be translated into tangible goals with a clear roadmap. This is strategic clarity.

Success Is Avoiding Failure

Approximately 70 percent of all strategies fail to achieve their intended goals. This is a frightening statistic. Imagine that instead of the long, difficult process of strategic thinking, you sell all your organization's assets, take the money, and place it on red at a roulette table in Las Vegas. The chance of walking out with a bigger pile of money is greater than achieving your strategic goals.

Strategic clarity is vital to improve upon the 70 percent failure rate. We have already identified several mistakes to avoid: being a Titanic organization, ignoring one or more steps of strategic thinking, executing the steps in the wrong sequence, and embracing a utopian vision.

Digging deeper, we encounter a fifth important reason strategies fail: a lack of execution power. Execution cannot occur in isolation. Strategic clarity requires a combination of having a vision and creating connections (Figure 2.1).

If an organization lacks both vision and connection, it is stuck. Failing organizations typically either have utopian visions that inspire people but do not connect with those who matter (clients, vendors, team members, and stakeholders), or they have no vision at all, resulting in a loss of execution power.

If an organization has a vision but lacks connection with the people necessary to make it happen, it operates from an Ivory Tower. This is a common issue when using strategy consultants. The strategy is developed in isolation without engagement between many of the senior leaders and the consultants. Once complete, it's communicated to the rest of the organization and stakeholders through endless slide decks and inspiring graphs. But since the people responsible for its execution were not consulted, a lot of energy is needed to bring them on board. Unfortunately, most of the organization's energy was spent on developing the strategy, leaving little for execution. As a result, the strategy fails to gain momentum.

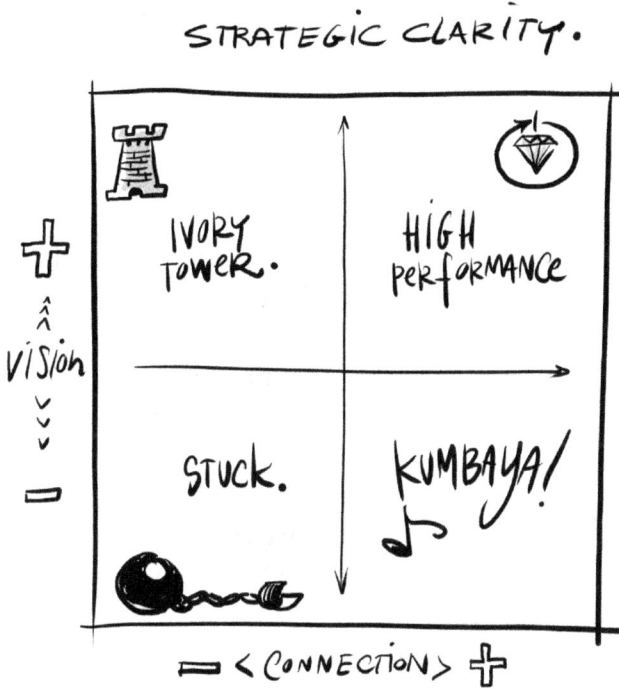

Figure 2.1 How to achieve strategic clarity

If there is connection but no vision, the organization becomes a "kumbaya" culture. Great teamwork and friendship are important, but without a vision, the organization becomes a group of friends without plans. This is often the result of ubiquitous team-building activities: They create better bonds but are useless without a powerful vision and inspirational goals.

Finally, when both vision and connection are present, the organization becomes high-performing.

Regardless of where you are in this matrix, what can you do to move to high performance? The first step is to avoid goal-setting mistakes.

Common Goal-Setting Mistakes

Business is about goals. All else is just commentary. A goal is the vector that brings a strategy to life. Goals are essential for business success, yet in my strategic work with clients, I have encountered eight consistent mistakes in strategic goal setting.

Mistake 1: Aspirational Goals Instead of Tangible Goals

Do you want to grow your business, accelerate innovation, or improve customer intimacy? Perhaps you do, but none of these are goals. These are aspirations. A goal is defined as something an external observer can clearly identify as achieved or not. It's always directional: moving from one specific state to another. Examples of good goals include increasing revenue from $100 to $110 million, or reducing the attrition rate from 4 percent to 3 percent. Every aspiration should be translated into a tangible goal. To do this, even with nontangible aspirations, ask yourself, What would an external observer notice if the aspirations were achieved? For example, if you aim to improve customer intimacy, ask what visible changes would indicate success, such as:

- Meeting agendas that incorporate the voice of the customer.
- A minimum amount of time spent with customers.
- An improvement in your Net Promoter Score (NPS) by a specific amount.

Mistake 2: "Meh" Goals Instead of Inspiring Goals

A good goal should inspire. When you imagine achieving it, there should be a sense of excitement. If you don't feel this, the goal is just "meh." The best goals are challenging, meaning there's a 50/50 chance of achieving them. If your team doesn't push back when discussing new goals, you probably aren't thinking big enough.

Mistake 3: Good Goals Instead of Best Goals

To gain clarity around goals, it's often more important to determine what a goal is not. Think of the best definition of a vacuum: the absence of matter. Or silence: the absence of noise. Similarly, the best way to define your goals is to define your "anti-goals." An anti-goal is a goal that is good but not the best. If your goal is to improve revenue, an anti-goal could be reducing costs. Reducing costs might be good, but not the best focus for your team. Creating an anti-goal list with your team is crucial for strategic clarity, as it helps maintain focus on what matters most.

Mistake 4: Important Goals Instead of Prioritized Goals

Imagine your top three goals are to grow revenue, increase quality, and accelerate innovation. When resources become scarce, you'll need to make choices. Your goal priorities will determine what gets sacrificed first. Being clear about your priorities ahead of time helps you and your team make better decisions.

Mistake 5: Individual Goals Instead of Common Goals

Individual goals must align with the team's common goals, and clarity on these common goals is essential. An effective approach to create alignment is to discuss with each team member how the team targets will help them to achieve their personal goals.

Mistake 6: Arbitrary Options Instead of Specific Goals

Say you want to accelerate innovation. You have several ways to achieve this goal. You can acquire a start-up, hire new talent, or set up a satellite innovation hub. You decide that the satellite hub is the best option. Proudly, you present it as part of the strategy. While this may demonstrate clarity and decisiveness, you've made a mistake. The satellite hub is just an option, not the goal. If the option becomes the goal, you've boxed yourself in. Many strategies fail because organizations confuse an option with a goal. The rule is: Be unyielding in your goals but flexible in your options.

Mistake 7: Project Thinking Instead of Portfolio Thinking

If you want to achieve a strategic goal but have no solution, you're stuck. If you have one solution, you have a problem. Two solutions give you a dilemma. Only with three or more solutions do you have flexibility. This is the essence of portfolio thinking. You develop as many options as possible to achieve your goal, starting with the most promising. If that option doesn't work out, move on to the next one. This keeps you flexible and resilient. Project thinking, on the other hand, is about being complete and accurate. It works for tasks like building a chemical plant, where a detailed project plan is necessary. However, in strategic thinking, portfolio thinking is the key to success.

Mistake 8: Boundaries Instead of Goals

A boundary is a condition that must be met under all circumstances; otherwise, your strategy fails. Boundaries can be implicit (e.g., following the law) or explicit (e.g., maintaining positive cash flow). Problems arise when boundaries are confused with strategic goals. For instance, if your quality performance is already good and no strategic initiatives are needed to improve it, quality is a boundary, not a goal. However, if strategic initiatives are necessary to improve quality due to new regulations, quality becomes a goal. To clarify boundaries, ask: "I have the freedom to do whatever it takes to achieve our strategic goals, provided that ...."

What You Need to Become

You've likely seen people make New Year's resolutions. Unfortunately, most of them fail. Why is it so hard to stick to resolutions and achieve goals? What's often missing is the clarification of good goals.

- It's not your goal; it's someone else's. True motivation comes from goals you're passionate about.
- The goal is too big, so it's rejected by the subconscious mind. Instead, make the goal smaller and more manageable.
- The goal is expressed negatively, such as "I will stop procrastinating." The subconscious mind struggles with negative statements, interpreting them as prompts to do the opposite. Always define goals in positive terms.

- Finally, to set effective goals, define what you need to become to achieve them. If you want to increase your team's innovation power, ask which behaviors and skills will help them most. Focus on traits like being comfortable with mistakes or improving external orientation. Then set specific goals to develop these behaviors and skills, one step at a time.

What's true for organizations is also true for individuals: People connect to organizational goals when they see what's in it for them. If a goal is too big, it's just a grand vision. Break it down into smaller, actionable steps.

Positive goals create more energy than avoiding negative outcomes. It's better to work toward a shining castle than to avoid a fiery pit.

Noses in the Same Direction

The new Berlin Brandenburg Airport became operational in May 2020. This beleaguered strategic project was completed almost a decade behind schedule and was four times more expensive than originally budgeted. In hindsight, this project failed because the preparation and design phase was too linear and too fast, leading to major issues during execution. Unfortunately, avoidable strategic project failures happen far too often.

The antidote to prevent failure and get all stakeholders aligned is to insist on conducting thorough Front End Loading (FEL). To set up an effective FEL, gather all stakeholders and discuss the following:

- What does project success look like? Define not only what success is but also what it isn't. For example, if your project involves building a new factory, marketing the product (the factory's output) may not be part of the scope.
- What aspects need to be considered to achieve success? Engage the group in a free-flow brainstorm to capture all the factors that need to be considered before executing the project. Use a prepared checklist to ensure completeness.
- What assumptions are critical for the success of the project?

- When should the project be abandoned? Set clear criteria for project abandonment, such as budget overruns or changes in critical assumptions. This avoids the sunk cost fallacy, where a doomed initiative is not stopped because too much time, money, and reputation have already been invested.

The FEL input serves as a solid foundation for a strong project plan to ensure smooth execution. A skilled carpenter knows something that many project managers have forgotten: "Measure twice, cut once."

Are Behavioral Standards Aligned?

Now that we've explored what needs to be eliminated to achieve strategic clarity, it's time to turn our attention to behavioral standards.

Predictable and consistent behavior is part of creating clarity. You don't want to operate in an organization where behavioral standards are inconsistent. Behaviors drive results, and erratic behaviors create erratic outcomes. Mindsets and behaviors form the foundation of a corporate culture. It's a big mistake to assume that everyone is on the same page behaviorally. While this may be true for implicit behaviors (e.g., following the law, not physically harming others), it's good practice to discuss explicit behavioral standards. This conversation starts with a simple question: "We are operating as a high-performance team when …."

Below is a checklist of behavioral focus areas. How do you want your team to behave regarding:

- Internal relations
- External relations
- Communicating bad news
- Celebrating wins
- Utilizing resources (including people)
- Adherence to processes
- Managing workload
- Setting priorities

Unleash Engagement with Creativity

Regardless of your strategic direction, engagement and connection with the rest of the organization are critical. While it may not be practical for everyone to be involved in the "why" and "what" of the strategy, everyone must play an important role in the "how." This requires tapping into the organization's creativity.

The typical way to do this is through a workshop-style session, such as a brainstorm. Most creative group sessions for brainstorming new ideas are ineffective: The usual output is a curious mix of circular reasoning, lack of imagination, and rehashed pet projects.

To avoid wasting your own precious time and others' limited energy, stick to the following best practices for your next brainstorm:

First, state the subject clearly at the beginning. The most powerful questions to get creative juices flowing is the Platinum Question consisting of three parts:

1. How can we ...
2. While at the same time ...
3. So that we ...

For example:

1. How can we speed up our project execution?
2. While at the same time staying within budget?
3. So that we improve our business case?

The first part helps frame the discussion and guide the brainstorming process. The second part establishes boundary conditions. Without clear boundaries, there are no useful ideas, only speculation. The third part of the Platinum Question describes the ultimate objective, allowing you to judge the validity of any idea.

Second, give all participants time to think: Let them generate ideas individually and in silence for at least 10 minutes.

Third, focus on quantity over quality: You need a lot of ideas to end up with a few good ones. To facilitate this, make abundant use of the Magic Question For Thinking Big (MQFTB): "What's even better than this?"

Fourth, define criteria for a "good" idea: At a minimum, a good idea must:

- Provide a solution to a significant issue.
- Be feasible.
- Be effective at solving the problem.
- Have more positives than negatives.

Fifth, close the session with a commitment for next steps:

- Provide a summary of the ideas.
- Describe a process to select the best ideas.
- Give clarity about any further expected involvement of participants.

Here are 10 ideas for a successful brainstorm session:

1. Parking Lot Magic: Park off-topic subjects separately and revisit them later.
2. Cone of Silence: What happens in the room stays in the room. Trust is key. If participants are afraid to speak due to hierarchy, use anonymous brainstorming (e.g., writing ideas on paper anonymously).
3. Musical Chairs: Swap seats at every break for fresh perspectives.
4. Time Boxing: Set fixed time slots for each topic (e.g., 15 minutes per topic).
5. Grim Reaper Rule: Silence means agreement. This ensures everyone takes ownership.
6. Going Supernova: After each idea, challenge the team with, "Can we top this?" to encourage thinking bigger.
7. Dragon Slayer: If consensus is reached too quickly on a difficult topic, dig deeper.
8. Idea Marathon: Generate at least 20 individual ideas before sharing with the group.

9. Silent Brainstorms: Quiet thinking for 10 minutes can spark brilliance, especially for introverted participants.
10. Action Finale: Conclude with crystal-clear steps—who does what and when.

Since the act of thinking requires a lot of energy, your brain develops automatic thinking patterns when faced with a problem. Getting new and original solutions is therefore difficult. The "20 ways thinking technique" helps bypass these mental barriers to keep generating new ideas. Here's how it works:

Define your problem as a question on a blank sheet of paper (e.g., How can I break the service standards in my industry?)

- Write down and number all the possible solutions to this problem.
- If the problem is significant, the first 5 to 10 solutions you write down will be obvious, as they are generated spontaneously by the conscious mind.
- Solutions 10 to 15 will be difficult because they require hard thinking and force you to create new associations. Your initial instinct will be to give up and name a previous solution as ideal. Don't give in to this instinct—continue.
- Solutions 15 to 20 are tough but force yourself to keep going. Oftentimes, the breakthrough insights and creative ideas come in the last five solutions.

The result of such a session is a strategic project portfolio: a list of options to achieve the organization's strategic goals. Next, you need to avoid mistakes in your structure to drive execution.

Optimization Requires Sacrifice

The French Maginot Line was designed as an impenetrable defense system against German tank divisions after World War I. However, when World War II started, the Germans simply circumvented the Maginot

Line with a fast tank push. The biggest mistake in war is preparing for the last one.

The same applies to strategies. New strategies fail because we organize ourselves to execute the previous one. As with war, changes in both the external and internal environment require us to adapt. The organizational principle for a new execution structure is to organize around the essential resources that are most limited—typically money, time, and quality. The law of strategic sacrifice dictates that you can only optimize two resources simultaneously; the third essential resource will fluctuate. This means a strategy or project can be:

- Good and cheap, but never fast: For example, hire and train internal resources to design and create a custom CRM system.
- Good and fast, but never cheap: Outsource the CRM project to an external company.
- Cheap and fast, but never good: Build your own CRM system using Excel.

Decide upfront which of the three is least painful to sacrifice. Then, focus on optimizing the other two. If you don't make this decision upfront, your strategy will likely be unsuccessful, expensive, and delayed—failure is imminent.

Strategic Clarity Blueprint

We have now arrived at the blueprint of strategic clarity.

This blueprint is the North Star for driving consistent execution. It answers the following questions:

- What does remarkable strategic success look like?
- What are our strategic goals?
- What are our anti-goals?
- What are the boundary conditions to stay within our strategy?
- What is our strategic portfolio with options to achieve our goals?
- What new behavioral standards do we need to set?
- How do we need to organize ourselves to drive execution?

This blueprint ensures that leaders will eliminate the tendency for their organization to operate from crisis to crisis. By taking out the clutter, it provides a powerful framework for accomplishing exponentially more by doing radically less.

Key Actionable Takeaways

1. **Eliminate the Habit of Crisis-Driven Leadership**: Stop relying on crises to drive focus and productivity. Instead, establish systems for prevention and clarity to ensure consistent progress without the need for emergency heroics.
2. **Remove Unrealistic, Utopian Visions**: Avoid visions that require massive sacrifices, defy human nature, or rely on improbable developments. Focus on achievable, inspiring goals that create optimism and joy.
3. **Discard Nontangible Aspirations**: Goals that cannot be measured or observed are distractions. Translate vague aspirations into specific, tangible objectives to provide clear direction and accountability.
4. **Cut Out Competing Priorities**: Overloaded goal lists dilute focus and resources. Identify and prioritize the most critical goals while eliminating lower-priority initiatives to ensure concentrated efforts on what matters most.
5. **Avoid Reactive Decision Making**: Eliminate impulsive, unstructured decisions during moments of pressure. Instead, predefine decision frameworks and boundary conditions to guide consistent, strategic choices.
6. **Stop Confusing Boundaries with Goals**: Ensure you differentiate between conditions (e.g., compliance with regulations) and true strategic objectives. Avoid treating boundaries as goals, which can misalign efforts.
7. **Remove Rigid, Single-Option Thinking**: Flexibility is essential for success. Eliminate a fixation on one path forward and adopt portfolio thinking to generate multiple solutions and maintain adaptability.
8. **Abandon Overcomplex Structures**: Streamline organizational systems and execution strategies. Remove unnecessary layers of complexity to ensure efficient, clear implementation of plans.

9. **Let Go of Resource Maximization Myths**: Acknowledge that you cannot optimize time, money, and quality simultaneously. Decide upfront which resource to sacrifice to focus on the other two.

10. **Eliminate the Busywork Trap**: Value deep thinking over constant activity. Remove nonessential tasks to create space for strategic thought and meaningful progress.

CHAPTER 3

Deep Impact

Ignore the Normal

How can you dramatically increase your impact without becoming obsessed with more–better–faster? The answer is to provide so much value that customers cannot help but work with your organization. Value creation is, therefore, a core responsibility for any leader. In this chapter, we will explore not only how business leaders can create value but especially how they can avoid common pitfalls that destroy value. To understand what drives value creation, we need to recognize that we live on two different planets: Steady Astra and Outlier Prime. Imagine humanity decides to journey to a planet called Steady Astra. Our spaceship, named *Steady Astra One*, has room for 100,000 people, selected from all of humanity by lottery, so we end up with a random selection of 100,000 individuals.

Let's take a closer look at one characteristic of these individuals—their proficiency in the high jump. Before entering the spaceship, every individual performs a jump and we analyze the results. Typically, we would observe two data points: First, there will be an average high jump result, perhaps around 1 m (3 ft). Second, the distribution will resemble a typical normal distribution, with extremes at the lower side (e.g., children) and the higher side (e.g., Olympic athletes). Now imagine we add one additional passenger: the world champion of the high jump. Though this individual is an outlier, achieving 2.10 m (6 ft), the impact on the average will be negligible. High jump performance, like height, weight, or IQ, resembles a normal distribution. Results are driven by the average, and outliers don't significantly impact the overall outcome. Thus, *Steady Astra One* is ruled by linear laws, where we typically find normal distributions in all variables.

The sister ship of *Steady Astra One* is called *Outlier Prime One*, and it also has a capacity of 100,000 passengers, selected randomly from all of humanity. Now, let's examine another characteristic of this group, wealth. The average wealth of the group is approximately $30,000. Now add the wealthiest person in the world as the 100,001st passenger. Currently, a few individuals are vying for the top spot, but generally, one of them would add some $200 billion to the mix. Suddenly, the average wealth jumps to more than $2 million per person on our spaceship. Wealth resembles a power distribution. Results are driven by outliers, and averages don't matter.

We see this power law everywhere. Some decades ago, while studying racehorse performance, scientists discovered a fascinating phenomenon: Over the long run, the number 1 racehorse earned up to 10 times more in prize money than the number 2 racehorse, even though it was less than 3 percent faster. They called this phenomenon the razor's edge—a small yet consistent advantage that results in an extremely large exponential positive effect on performance and success. The razor's edge is not limited to horse racing; it applies equally to modern businesses and professionals. The secret to creating impact is to do a few things slightly differently to create small advantages in key areas. It's pointless to slightly improve activities that operate under Steady Astra principles; it will hardly make a difference. However, improving activities that operate under Outlier Prime principles can be incredibly valuable. This is the key to significantly improving value creation. It requires that we stop trying to improve the normal and leverage all our energy on outliers.

Maximum Leadership Leverage

Which organizational activities provide the maximum leadership leverage? Figure 3.1 shows how an organization spends its energy:

- Duct Tape Management: Issues are resolved, but they resurface repeatedly. Rinse and repeat. Think of a dysfunctional process that requires constant manual intervention.
- Problem-Solving: Issues are solved in a straightforward manner.
- Operations: These are all the activities necessary to run your current business.

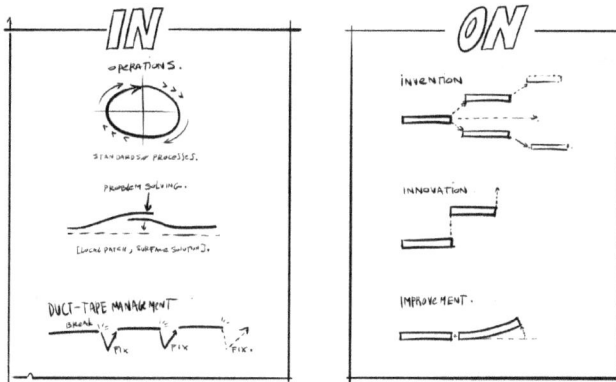

Figure 3.1 Energy Shift: the six areas where an organization spends its energy

- Improvement: Activities that gradually create a better version of a process or system, such as company-wide Six Sigma initiatives or automation. Note that improvement only occurs if it sets you apart from the competition. For example, in the chemical industry, a standard rule is that fixed costs must be reduced by 3 percent every year just to keep up with the competition. Only activities that exceed this baseline are true improvement activities.
- Innovation: Introducing new approaches from outside the organization to create additional value.
- Invention: Developing completely new services or products that open new markets and attract new customers.

Duct tape management, problem-solving, and operations are activities within the "working *in* the business" bucket. Improvement, innovation, and invention are activities within the "working *on* the business" bucket. All activities within the "working in the business bucket" have a ceiling on their potential impact. For example, cost-cutting: The maximum impact of cost-cutting is when all costs are eliminated, but at that point, you won't have any business left either. Moreover, achieving the same level of impact becomes exponentially more difficult—for instance, reducing costs by 5 percent requires a certain amount of resources, but the next 5 percent often requires significantly more.

On the other hand, all activities within the "working on the business" bucket have no ceiling. The same effort can yield exponential results. For instance, a new product can attract one new customer or thousands of new customers. Working in the business operates under Steady Astra principles. Working on the business operates under Outlier Prime principles.

You can accelerate your impact if you leverage your own activities and those of your organization to transition from working in the business to working on the business. Let's explore leadership strategies to eliminate everything that prevents you from working on the business.

The Wrong Type of Innovation

Imagine you own an old computer, and its speed is limited by its amount of random access memory (RAM). If you replace the computer's processor, you increase its potential; you create the possibility that it will be faster in the future. However, if you increase its RAM, you improve its performance. The effects and benefits of this action are immediate. The distinction between increasing performance versus potential is crucial if you want to rapidly move to high performance. A big trap in business is that significant energy, time, and money are often spent on what could be, rather than on immediate improvements (Figure 3.2).

If your organization is underperforming versus its potential, focus on innovation that improves capturing value. If your organization is overperforming versus its potential, focus on innovation to expand value. For example, a typical mistake of choosing potential over performance is

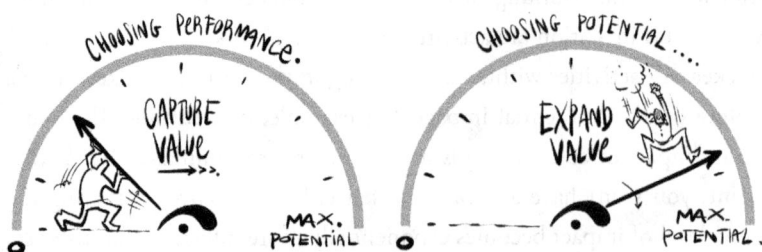

Figure 3.2 Performance versus potential: what to focus on in order to create value

deciding to invest in future production capacity without market demand, assuming that if you invest in it, the results will follow. They seldom do.

On the other hand, it's a mistake to choose performance over potential by continuing to train people in improving current skills instead of future skills needed for emerging technology. Becoming better at something which will be irrelevant in the near future is a waste of time, money, and energy. The distinction between performance and potential will help you choose the right innovation focus for your organization.

Ignoring the Outside World

Over 300 people disappear yearly on cruises due to suicides, crimes, accidents, or deliberate plans to vanish. Few of us likely knew this, but we simply accept it as part of that specific industry. Decades ago, it was accepted that the heavy chemical industry was an extremely dangerous place to work. Due to regulations, company focus, new technology, and public pressure, worker deaths have been significantly reduced; workplace fatalities are now an exception rather than the rule.

Almost every industry or profession has internal standards, which may be the norm for insiders but are unfamiliar to outsiders. These internal standards can lead to innovation in other industries. Every industry or profession is exposed to a process I call professional osmosis: Better standards in the external world will eventually become part of your own world as well. From this perspective, innovation is the deliberate process of speeding up the adoption of new and better standards in your industry or profession to match the higher standards of the external world. Overcoming myopic thinking and driving professional osmosis starts with a decision: Which low internal standard in your workplace will you no longer accept?

Chasing Shiny Objects

Right now, AI is all the rage and massive resources are pouring into this new technology. Yet it's a story that has been repeated many times. In the past two decades, we've seen an ever-changing focus on finding the next shiny object: Digitalization, sustainability, big data, and others have all been part of a long list of breakthrough subjects. It's a mistake to think that simply understanding and embracing these popular topics will drive innovation in your organization. Since everyone else is also focused on AI, sustainability, digitalization, and big data, these are now just considered necessary factors to stay in business. Thus, any innovation strategy based solely on what's new ad popular will result in a poor imitation, identical to those produced by other unimaginative competitors. An innovation strategy is only effective if it sets you apart. Otherwise, it's just business maintenance. The best innovations happen behind the scenes. What are you quietly working on that will truly make a difference for your future clients?

In Love with Scientism

In the fictional Warhammer universe, there is a human faction called the Techpriests. They are obsessed with technology, and their main objective is to become one with their Machine God. To achieve this transformation, they systematically replace the biological parts of their bodies with bizarre cybernetics. This reminds me of scientism: replacing something that works well with something that works on paper, all in the name of progress. Examples include replacing perfectly functional physical buttons in cars with tablet-like screens, substituting local decision making with top-down 5-year Soviet-style plans, or using model simulations instead of real-world observations. In organizations, scientism often adds layers of complexity, slows down operations, and dilutes the focus on achieving big goals.

How do you distinguish between scientism and innovation? I have found that you're dealing with scientism if a replacement:

- Does not improve speed, quality, or value in the eyes of the majority of end-users or clients.
- Requires additional and consistent upgrades or maintenance to keep working.
- Performs a function that shouldn't be done at all.
- Can only be changed by external specialists.
- Outsources critical thinking to a system.
- Triggers shortcuts and exceptions to make it work.
- Far exceeds the technology level of the rest of the organization.

- Provides external bragging rights to senior executives.
- Requires vague selling points, such as compliance, sustainability, or progress.
- Is not immediately intuitive for the uninitiated.
- Can't be tested on a small scale.

Never use the utopian approach of scientism to avoid working on real innovation.

Getting Unstuck

If you do what everyone else is doing, you're not distinguishing yourself from the competition, and you're probably stuck. Here are 10 ideas to do things differently and get unstuck:

- Create artificial scarcity: Booking.com always claims there are only a few rooms left.
- Use the negative aspect of your product as an asset: The controversial taste of Red Bull signals sacrifice to improve performance.
- Understand what is grudgingly accepted in your market by everyone else and change it: Robinhood introduced no-fee stock trading.
- Break industry norms: IKEA lets customers build their own furniture.
- Emulate the business values of your ideal client: John Deere works with independent dealers to support independent farmers.
- Take out steps: Dell has removed brick-and-mortar stores.
- Make it bigger: iPad Pro.
- Make it smaller: iPad Mini.
- Make it faster: flash delivery for groceries.
- Make it slower: slow food.

Notice Countertrends

While enjoying the summer holidays in Italy, we decided to buy some fresh, delicious focaccia. When I went to pay, I noticed a big black box humming at the register: It was a state-of-the-art payment machine that took cash as input at the top and returned change at the bottom. This was interesting: Societies are rapidly moving toward cashless transactions, yet here was a brand-new machine explicitly designed to facilitate and improve cash payments. This follows the boomerang rule in business: For every trend, there will be a countertrend. For example, despite the growth of digital services like Spotify, sales of vinyl records have increased by more than 100 percent in the past year. Businesses operating in the vinyl niche are doing very well. Sometimes it's a good idea to unfollow trends to avoid the trap of more–better–faster. Leave the herd, and you may find the grass is indeed greener on the other side.

Underserved and Unhappy Clients

In 1521, the mighty Aztec Empire fell just 2 years after Spanish conquistador Hernando Cortés made first contact. His army had fewer than 600 soldiers. How was his victory possible? The superior weaponry of the Spanish played a major role. The unintentional introduction of European diseases was also a significant factor. Yet there was a third reason. The brutality of the Aztecs toward their conquered neighbors made those neighbors quickly rally around the Spanish flag when Cortés arrived in 1519. This resulted in an avalanche of opposing forces, and the outcome was inevitable. The avalanche of opposing forces occurs when strange bedfellows find a common cause—usually a mutual enemy. The rapid rise of Uber in many big cities can be explained by deep customer dissatisfaction with a monopolized and abusive taxi system that had lost its focus on its customers. Disruption isn't triggered by new technology but by unhappy clients who are forcefully deprived of choice. Which unhappy clients are currently underserved?

Effective Is Not Enough

Some time ago, I traveled by Eurostar from Brussels to London. Using the underground tunnel to cross the English Channel by train was, overall, a fascinating and pleasant experience. But in order to check in, I had to join a long queue, put my luggage through a scanner, join another long queue for border control, find a seat in a crowded and boring waiting area, and join another queue to finally board the train. All of this reminded me of taking a plane. And not in a good way. The frustrating part of flying is often the check-in and boarding process. Therefore, it's strange that the Eurostar train, which competes with air travel, has adopted the same inefficiencies. Instead of creating an opportunity to stand out and delight passengers, they chose to adopt a process that, though functional and based on best practices in air travel, results in a negative user experience. We can all benefit from using our creativity to challenge our systems. However, any innovation in our systems should not only be effective, it should also be remarkable.

The Big Issue with Scalability

Richard Feynman, the eminent physicist, once said that things on a very small scale behave like nothing that you have any direct experience with. He was referring to the bizarre world of quantum mechanics, where an electron can be everywhere all at once, light can be either a particle or a wave, and paired particles can synchronize instantaneously regardless of distance. The very small is totally different from the very large—the system is nonfractal.

Fractal structures are irregular geometrical shapes that appear similar regardless of the level of magnification. For example, a grain of salt looks like a rock when magnified, and looks like a mountain when magnified even further. The distinction between fractal and nonfractal is important if you want to introduce best practices to optimize and scale an organization. A best practice will only be effective when dealing with a fractal system but may hopelessly fail when dealing with a nonfractal system. This is the big issue with macroeconomics: It is a nonfractal system where the small (e.g., individual behavior) is very different from the big (e.g., government behavior). Yet we often assume they are governed by the same laws.

The signs that you are dealing with a nonfractal system, where scaling best practices may not be effective, are:

- A large number of stakeholders with competing goals and objectives.

- Winner-takes-all dynamics: A few activities, processes, or products are essential and capture almost all value.
- Exponential impact of risk: Spilling a drop of a chemical may be harmless; spilling a tank load of the same chemical may be disastrous.

All of these magnify structural weaknesses in any system you want to scale. Be careful with mindlessly copying best practices to innovate: What works in a neat, controlled environment may lead to ruin when applied on a larger scale.

The Benefits of Cutting Resources

In economics, there is a concept known as the Laffer curve. It illustrates the relationship between the total tax revenue of a government and the tax rate. The extremes of the curve demonstrate that at a 0 percent tax rate, tax revenues will be zero. Similarly, at a 100 percent tax rate, few people would be willing to work, leading government tax revenue to also drop to zero. This suggests there is an optimal tax rate at which a government's tax revenue is maximized. Increasing the tax rate beyond this optimal point actually decreases tax revenue. This idea can also be applied to organizations. There is a point at which adding more resources, such as people or money, will no longer improve results. In fact, the opposite occurs: Results decrease. Approximately 30 percent of all resources in U.S. health care are used for administration. With more and more administrative resources being added to the system every year, this percentage has been increasing without a similar increase in patient care outcomes. The same trend applies to higher education, where administrative costs now account for up to 40 percent of total expenditure. I call this phenomenon Terminal Bureaucracy (Figure 3.3).

This figures illustrates that at a certain point, complexity becomes rampant, and adding more resources decreases results. If you find yourself facing Terminal Bureaucracy in your organization, you may be pleasantly surprised to see what happens when you cut resources.

GROW   STRUGGLE   DIMINISH   COLLAPSE

PERFORMANCE.

ADDING RESOURCES →.

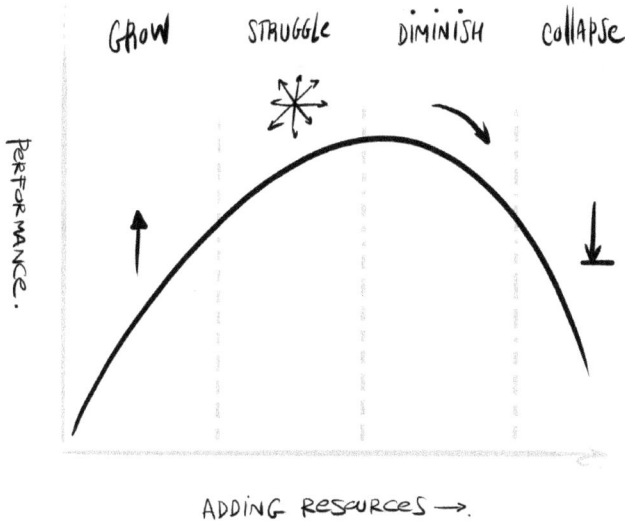

Figure 3.3 Terminal Bureaucracy: the impact of adding resources to organizational performance

Stop Fighting Entropy

Entropy is the general trend toward disorder. This is true not only for natural systems but also for human endeavors and organizations. The second law of thermodynamics states that entropy always increases over time. Many things we intensely disliked in the past slowly creep back into our lives. Take, for example, YouTube. When it was introduced in 2005, we finally had the freedom to choose our entertainment whenever we wanted, circumventing the hated commercials on TV. Fast forward 20 years and commercials have made a glorious comeback on YouTube. Another example is the average speed of traffic in big cities, which is declining. In London, it's now less than 25 km/h (15 mph)—not much faster than traveling in the city with a horse-drawn carriage in the nineteenth century.

Much of our professional attention is absorbed simply by fighting entropy to maintain the status quo. We create better computer interfaces to compensate for slower processes caused by ever-growing rules. We hold more meetings to tackle a growing lack of alignment between teams. We hire more people to audit and check the work of others. It's time to take a radical approach. Instead of compensating for entropy, focus your energy on changing the system. Eliminate everything that creates complexity, increases frustration, or reduces speed for you and your team. A slower process doesn't need a better interface—it needs a wrecking ball.

Key Actionable Takeaways

1. **Eliminate "Normal" Improvements**: Stop focusing on marginal gains in areas governed by average outcomes (Steady Astra principles). Instead, channel your efforts toward activities with exponential potential, where small changes lead to massive impact.
2. **Cut Out Duct Tape Management**: Remove reliance on temporary fixes that repeatedly address the same issues. Prioritize sustainable solutions that permanently resolve problems and free resources for strategic innovation.
3. **Stop Chasing Shiny Objects**: Avoid investing in trendy technologies or ideas that fail to differentiate your organization. Focus instead on under-the-radar innovations that create true competitive advantage.
4. **Remove Overemphasis on Potential at the Expense of Performance**: Don't overinvest in future possibilities while neglecting immediate value creation. Balance your efforts to optimize current results while strategically expanding for the future.
5. **Eliminate Scientism**: Avoid replacing effective processes with overly complicated systems that add no tangible value. Simplify operations by focusing on what enhances speed, quality, or client satisfaction.
6. **Trim Terminal Bureaucracy**: Reduce unnecessary administrative overhead that diminishes efficiency and results. Streamline processes and reclaim resources for high-impact activities.
7. **Let Go of Entropy-Induced Layers**: Stop adding layers to counteract inefficiencies caused by organizational complexity. Focus instead on removing the root causes of disorder to accelerate performance and alignment.

8. **Stop Fighting Trends Mindlessly**: Don't blindly follow industry norms or trends. Instead, seek opportunities in countertrends that challenge conventional approaches and uncover hidden value.

9. **Abandon Overly Complex Scalability Plans**: Remove scalability strategies that fail to consider the unique dynamics of nonfractal systems. Focus on scaling only what aligns with your core competencies and success factors.

10. **Reduce Resource Reliance to Spark Creativity**: Cut excess resources to encourage innovative problem-solving. Lean operations often lead to sharper focus, agility, and breakthrough solutions.

CHAPTER 4

Extraordinary Leadership

Extreme Ownership

Hannibal Barca, the famous Carthaginian general, was the nemesis of ancient Rome. In 218 BC, he concocted a daring plan to enter his enemy's heartland—Italy. A key element of his army was his contingent of war elephants. Enormous and ferocious, they had the ability to frighten and thwart cavalry charges and steamroll infantry. The problem, however, was that the elephants needed to cross the high peaks of the Alps. His generals came to him in desperation, asking how to manage this seemingly impossible task. His answer? "I will find a way, or make one." Hannibal was a tough cookie—the Vin Diesel of ancient times.

I call this straightforward approach to problem-solving the Hannibal Mindset. It represents extreme ownership, and we will see that this is a very important key to effective leadership.

But what is ownership? It's a mistake to think that ownership means always committing to the uncontrollable. It means that, regardless of the circumstances, you keep asking yourself: What action can we take that will have a positive influence on the desired outcome? It means taking ownership of what you can control, stretching yourself to expand your influence, and ignoring what you can't control.

Ownership for leaders starts with deciding what not to focus on. It's a waste of time to work on things you can neither control nor influence. This is an obvious point, yet often forgotten. I have seen too many strategies depend on external events, such as economic growth. This brings us back to the illusion of control.

The Ownership Ladder

Let's now assess the ownership mindset of your organization or team. The greater the ownership mindset the better the results. If every individual in an organization is constantly focused on what they can do to create a positive impact, it creates forward momentum. The opposite of the owner mindset creates a victimhood mentality. The two extremes are part of a ladder (Figure 4.1).

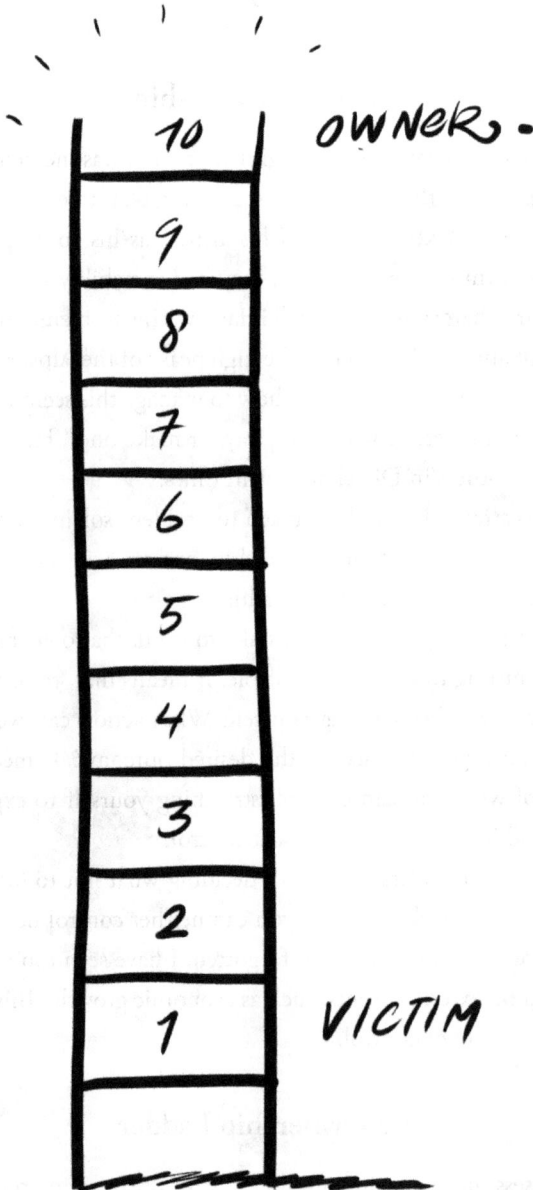

Figure 4.1 The Ownership Ladder

Where would you place your team on this ladder? Regardless of the score, climbing the ownership ladder will make you more effective. This requires eliminating victimhood.

We can recognize victimhood in two areas: language and activities.

The language of victimhood is very specific:

- "I can't because of my boss, my education, the rules ..."
- "I have to because of my boss, my education, the rules ..."
- "I deserve because of my boss, my education, the rules ..."

The organizational mechanism that accelerates this mindset is called Learned Helplessness.

Elephant trainers in India have a specific way of creating obedience. A young elephant calf is tied with a rope to a stake in the ground. It quickly learns that its freedom is limited to the length of the rope. As it grows older, it becomes so used to the limits of the rope that it doesn't realize it can simply break free by force. It creates a prison of its own making.

Typical characteristics of teams and organizations that have fallen prey to Learned Helplessness include:

- Advancement is based on who you are, not what you've done.
- Decision making is moved upward as much as possible.
- Career development is the responsibility of the Human Resources department.
- Performance reviews happen once a year, with no follow-up.
- Structural underperformance is widespread and tacitly accepted.
- Top performers are looked down upon, and underperformance is quickly normalized by peer pressure.
- Problem-solving is done by committee.
- Key problems are managed, not solved.
- Low attrition of mediocre performers.
- Difficulty in attracting top talent.
- Seniority and credentials trump competence.

Avoiding Victimhood

A culture of full ownership is essential if you want your organization to achieve much more by doing much less. It means that people are focused on what they can do to drive progress and resolve issues. To achieve this, we first need to understand what doesn't work when trying to drive ownership. Avoid everything that creates Learned Helplessness and Splendid Unaccountability.

The first unhelpful approach is telling people to show more ownership. Simply giving this message at the next performance management meeting is useless. Long workshops or town halls diving into the philosophy behind ownership assume that people lack the skill to take ownership, which is rarely true. The problem isn't a lack of skills—it's a mindset issue.

The second unhelpful approach is relying on motivational posters proclaiming that "Ownership is the lifeblood of our future." Frequent, in-your-face triggers don't change behavior, and they can lead to subconscious resentment, sometimes resulting in the opposite behavior.

The third unhelpful approach is amateur psychology. This involves psychobabble where people are invited to search their past for the root cause of victimhood behavior. Leaders shouldn't act as psychologists. If the problem is rooted in childhood trauma, mental health professionals should be consulted.

An organizational culture is set by its senior leaders. If you encounter high levels of victimhood, ask yourself a deeply uncomfortable but essential question: "What is it in my behavior that triggers victimhood in others instead of ownership?"

Ignore the Bat-Signal

Marvel movies are hugely entertaining: The adventures of Thor, Iron Man, and the Guardians of the Galaxy are an endless source of amusement. There's a subtle message hidden in this standard Marvel plot: Solving problems, being heroic, and saving the day is the path to success. This works well for entertainment but fails when building high-performance teams.

When I first led a small team of engineers, I thought my role was to solve their problems so they could focus on work. I felt like a true Marvel hero. Yet, after a few weeks, my boss pointed out that he had hired me to lead like a fire captain, but I was acting like a firefighter instead. I had to change course.

Heroic leaders love to step in and solve problems whenever the Bat-Signal appears in the sky. However, they forget that the most important job of a leader is to create an environment where their team members take ownership and solve problems themselves. This is how organizations grow and people develop. The secret to creating ownership is to become a hero catalyst. We measure a leader's effectiveness by how many heroes they create in their organization.

A big red flag pointing to a heroic leadership culture that promotes victimhood is Executive Babysitting. Leaders who are part of this culture spend enormous amounts of time in the following roles:

- The Referee: Instead of solving issues among themselves, team members engage the leader to mediate conflicts.
- The Taskmaster: Leaders chase deadlines, KPIs, and reports for others, turning into glorified personal assistants.
- The Monkey Magnet: Team members bring their problems (= monkeys) to the leader to solve, leaving the leader with additional issues and team members who are unable to handle their own problems.

The root cause of these behaviors is that team members have learned to outsource their own thinking to you. Therefore, the solution is straightforward: Force people to start thinking for themselves again. Never allow anyone to present a problem or dispute without also presenting multiple solutions. This simple principle will result in the vast majority of problems being solved before they reach your desk. This behavioral standard—being a hero versus creating heroes—is critical for driving ownership. Let's look at other behavioral leadership standards that drive out victimhood.

Playing to Win Versus Playing Not to Lose

Are you playing to win or playing not to lose? Imagine watching a sports game between two teams. You are unfamiliar with both teams but decide to enjoy the game anyway. After a short while, you realize that one team is stalling, playing defensively, and afraid of taking risks. The second team, on the other hand, plays with urgency, is on the offensive, and attacks whenever possible. One team is playing not to lose, while the other is playing to win.

This distinction is very important: Our natural instinct is to be attracted to the team that is playing to win.

What's true for sports is true for organizations and individuals. When Uber arrived on the scene, the default reaction of most existing taxi companies was lawfare—using legal strategies to bar this upstart from entering the market. They were playing not to lose. Ironically, when one taxi company decided to go on strike to protest Uber, it provided a boon for Uber to attract many new clients.

A typical situation of a leader playing not to lose is when they are "hijacked." Not long ago, a client lamented the glaring underperformance of a sales executive. She confessed that firing him would mean risking his key customers leaving with him. That's when it hit me: She was a hijacked leader. Hijacked leaders have the formal authority to make tough decisions but are shackled in decision making by their own people.

How do you spot a hijacked leader? First, underperformance isn't just visible—it's glaring, yet mysteriously tolerated. Second, rule-breaking runs rampant without objection. What is most curious is that hijacked leaders have built a mental prison of their own making. The fear of facing the negative consequences of a tough decision means they are playing not to lose, instead of playing to win. The only solution to this situation is to have the courage to bite the bullet and strategically minimize its downside. My client decided to jump into the mouth of the tiger. The sales executive was let go. Some key clients drifted away, but the business didn't just survive—it sailed toward unprecedented success with its captain back in control.

How do you ensure your team plays to win? Sometimes it's tempting to apply a cheat code, what video gamers refer to as God Mode. It means you're invulnerable, have unlimited resources, and can dominate the gameplay. I once played the game "Wolfenstein" in God Mode. At first, it was magnificent to "stride the battlefield like a Titan of ancient times." But very quickly, it became … boring. There was no challenge, no excitement, and no fun. I have never played in God Mode again. In life, we need challenges, setbacks, and disappointments to appreciate victories and achievements. Nothing could be more bland than a work environment that is totally predictable, uneventful, and lacks volatility.

Let's stop trying to operate in God Mode and challenge ourselves and our team to break the good and create the better. Life's excitement, progress, and innovation are driven by pushing against constraints. If a dysfunctional team plays in God Mode and is consistently rewarded with more resources, the Pavlovian response is to create more dysfunction to obtain even more resources. As leaders, we must break this cycle. Limit resources because unlimited resources dull the mind.

Agreements Versus Expectations

Imagine you need to have the leaking roof of your warehouse repaired. You consider two different companies to solve this pressing issue. Company A drops by, assesses the situation, and tells you that the repair cost and timeline are unclear. But, if you give them a green light, they will start working you into their schedule. Company B, on the other hand, conducts a thorough inspection and provides a detailed quote with cost, timeline, and guarantees. Naturally, company B is the obvious choice. The main issue is no longer if you can get it cheaper; the main issue is trust. The two behaviors that drive trust are consistency and reliability. That's why the distinction between agreements and expectations is so important.

An agreement has four components:

1. Clarity: It must be crystal clear.
2. Time-specific: When will it be completed?
3. Mutual: All parties must accept it.
4. Escalation process: If circumstances change and the agreements can no longer be fulfilled, how do we respond? Do we ignore the issue or proactively reach out to see what can be salvaged?

A company culture based on expectations instead of agreements quickly earns the stigma of being unreliable. This is deadly. This doesn't mean that every expectation must be replaced with agreements. It means that as leaders, we need to eliminate those expectations that undermine reliability and consistency in our teams.

Serving Versus Pleasing

On January 27, 1986, Thiokol engineers and managers discussed the weather conditions surrounding the upcoming launch of the Space Shuttle Challenger with their counterparts from NASA. The weather was very cold, and one of the design engineers, Roger Boisjoly, pointed out the negative impact of low temperatures on the reliability of the rubber O-rings that sealed the fuel rocket joints. He recommended a launch postponement. His bosses, however, refused to take that recommendation to NASA leadership. As a result, on January 28, the Challenger exploded only 73 seconds after launch, caused by a failed O-ring.

Sugarcoating difficult messages to keep the peace and avoid confrontation might make people happy in the short term, but it's devastating for long-term success. For example, people-pleasing typically happens during interactions with customers. After all, you want to make them happy. Yet by playing the yes-man, you may miss an opportunity to really serve your customers. Where is your team focused on people pleasing when it should be focused on serving instead?

Curious Versus Convinced

As a young doctor in Vienna, Ignaz Semmelweis observed that the habit of handwashing among medical staff significantly decreased the mortality rate of women giving birth in the hospital. Since bacteria would not be discovered by Louis Pasteur until decades later, Semmelweis was unable to scientifically explain his findings and, as a result, was scorned by the established medical community. Instead of gaining accolades, his standing among his peers was literally washed away. He spent the last weeks of his tragic life in a mental hospital, driven mad by his inability to instill simple hygiene habits that could have saved many lives.

The Semmelweis reflex is a metaphor for the rejection of new knowledge because it contradicts existing norms, beliefs, or paradigms. This typically happens when empirical data contradicts broadly accepted scientific theories or business practices. Progress in science and business always starts by challenging current thinking. Thus, any advancement slows down when we no longer allow certain parts of our knowledge to be questioned, especially when it disrupts the political power structure. Science is never settled.

The same is true for organizations. Innovation halts when politics and power become more important than progress and curiosity. That's why you should never mix politics and business—politics blocks creative thinking in organizations. Leaders need to recognize the difference between being curious and being convinced. To avoid the Semmelweis reflex and engage in new thinking, ask yourself with an open mind: What is working remarkably well in our organization, which shouldn't be working at all?

Principles Versus Taste

A principle is a condition that must be met under all circumstances. Any deviations are unacceptable. Taste is a condition that elicits preferences, but you can accept a suboptimal condition. The distinction between principles and taste drives empowerment and ownership.

More than 2,300 years ago, Philip II of Macedon—the father of Alexander the Great—became Strategos Autokrator of the League of Corinth: the first federation of Greek States. The title meant that he had the freedom to do what it took to advance the interests of the Hellenic states, while at the same time, remaining accountable for his actions. This ancient approach to leadership is still useful today. When you want to grow as a leader, more tasks must be delegated to others. After all, your time is a limited resource.

This requires three steps:

1. Clearly define what the task needs to accomplish. Don't tell people what to do, but explain what the outcome of their work needs to be.
2. Set the boundaries for the desired outcome. Think of timeline, budget, resources, and so forth.
3. Be very clear about what you expect your people to do if one of those boundaries is in jeopardy. For example: "If you find that you run the risk of not making the timeline, I want you to inform me immediately so we can adapt accordingly."

Figure 4.2 The Sandbox: how to create ownership in your team

This approach is called the Sandbox: It defines the field in which your team can play (Figure 4.2).

The borders of the Sandbox are determined by the following statement: "You have all the freedom to do whatever it takes, provided that …."

Thus, the Sandbox helps create as much freedom as possible by giving your people as few rules as possible. At the same time, hold your people vigorously, consistently, and visibly accountable for following these rules.

Catalyst Versus Kryptonite

A catalyst is a substance that accelerates a chemical reaction but is not consumed in the process. For example, iron acts as a catalyst in the Haber–Bosch process to make ammonia. Catalyst behaviors accelerate the strength of any leader.

Kryptonite is a fictional substance from the Superman universe. Superman was strong and powerful, but as soon as he was close to Kryptonite, he lost all his powers. Kryptonite behaviors mask your strengths as a leader.

Most of us are familiar with the Golden Rule: "Do unto others as you would have them do unto you." However, an even more important rule for high-performance leadership is the Silver Rule: "Do not do to others what you would not want others to do to you." The Golden Rule focuses on doing good, while the Silver Rule focuses on preventing harm.

Applying the Silver Rule keeps us humble, thoughtful, and empathetic. Often, we are so enamored with our own ideas and initiatives that we forget the negative impact of our behaviors on others. The practical application of the Silver Rule is to eliminate our own Kryptonite behaviors.

There are several specific areas where applying the Silver Rule makes us better human beings in a professional environment:

"Yes, but …": This phrase means that you can ignore everything before the word "but." It's much more effective to use "Yes, and …" or simply say no.

Adding too much value: A few years ago, I decided to buy a new television. I did my research and found the model I wanted online. To support the local economy, I went to the neighborhood electronics shop to buy it. Instead of making an easy sale, the enthusiastic sales professional began explaining all the features and technical details. After 10 minutes, I cut him short, went home, and bought the TV online. This is called adding too much value. In an attempt to impress others, people provide so much information that they become annoying. A simple technique to avoid this trap is to pause, take a breath, and ask if you should continue. Sometimes, the best way to improve effectiveness is to simply stop talking.

Listening to reply: People who listen only to respond can't wait to monopolize the conversation and introduce their own point of view. This behavior is infuriating. Listen to understand instead.

Preemptive excuses: Have you ever heard someone say, "I don't want to be rude, but …"? It's usually followed by something rude. Preemptive excuses allow unacceptable behavior. This is unprofessional and conveys amateurism. Think of a speaker who starts by saying, "I'm not a good speaker." Instead of delighting the audience, it fills them with dread.

Negativity: If your default response to new ideas is to explain why they won't work, you will create an environment where no one brings you new ideas. Negativity kills drive. It's the difference between being curious and being convinced.

Winner's obsession: When I was a student, I joined the debating team and soon applied those skills to my social circle. Three months later, I didn't have a social circle left. Winner's obsession means treating everything as a duel to be won. This behavior is toxic and quickly repels people.

Right at all costs: In 2006, the International Astronomical Union (IAU) demoted Pluto from planet to "dwarf planet." Technically, this was the right decision, but emotionally, it created resentment. Being right is not the same as being effective. Do you want to be right, or do you want to be effective?

Unfiltered verbalization: King Henry II of England once said, "Will no one rid me of this troublesome priest?" Four knights interpreted this as a command and murdered Thomas Becket in Canterbury Cathedral. Leaders must be careful with unfiltered speech; it may be interpreted as a command, instead of opening a conversation.

Exaggerated language: "He never listens." "She's always late." "No one takes initiative." "Everyone disagrees." These are examples of exaggerated language. Exaggeration steers conversations in the wrong direction and makes discussions defensive. Use precise language and specific examples to help people improve. For instance, "This report is not up to your usual standards of precision" is more constructive than "You're always sloppy."

Passive yet Aggressive

A telltale sign of organizational decline is the erosion of human civility. Many uncivil behaviors, such as ad hominem attacks, rudeness, or public cursing, are obvious. Less obvious is passive-aggressive behavior, where negative feelings are expressed indirectly instead of openly. Some examples of passive-aggressive behaviors may be familiar to you:

- Backhanded compliments: "This is well-done. Did you finally raise your working standards?"
- Ignoring others' success.
- Nonresponse to e-mails and phone calls.
- Cynical remarks: "We work for the boss's bonus."

Passive-aggressive behavior drains organizational energy. If you encounter passive-aggressive behavior, immediately address it head-on: "That wasn't a helpful remark. Why would you say something like that?"

The simple act of maintaining civility is like installing snow guards on your roof. They prevent a slow trickle of bad behavior from turning into a disastrous avalanche.

Key Actionable Takeaways

1. **Let Go of the Illusion of Control**: Stop focusing on external factors beyond your influence, such as economic conditions or market trends. Redirect energy toward areas where your actions can make a tangible impact.
2. **Eliminate Heroic Leadership**: Avoid being the default problem-solver. Step back and empower team members to resolve issues themselves, fostering a culture of ownership and independence.
3. **Cut Out Victimhood Language**: Eradicate phrases like "I can't" or "I have to" from team conversations. Replace them with proactive language that emphasizes control, accountability, and progress.
4. **Stop Supporting Learned Helplessness**: Remove practices that encourage dependency, such as decision making by committee or top-down mandates. Promote autonomy by decentralizing decision making and valuing initiative.
5. **Avoid Executive Babysitting**: Stop acting as a referee or taskmaster for your team. Instead, establish systems where team members manage conflicts and meet deadlines without constant oversight.
6. **Abandon Resource Overload**: Limit resources deliberately to encourage innovation and creative problem-solving. Excess resources often dull critical thinking and foster inefficiency.
7. **Eliminate Passive-Aggressive Behaviors**: Address indirect negativity, such as backhanded compliments or silent resistance, directly and constructively. These behaviors erode trust and team cohesion.
8. **Stop Adding Complexity to Agreements**: Clarify expectations by replacing vague assumptions with clear, time-specific agreements. This ensures reliability and reduces ambiguity across the team.

9. **Get Over the Need to Be Right**: Stop prioritizing correctness over effectiveness. Shift focus to achieving meaningful outcomes rather than winning arguments.

10. **Minimize Negativity Toward New Ideas**: Remove the tendency to reject ideas prematurely. Cultivate curiosity and encourage team members to explore possibilities, driving innovation and growth.

CHAPTER 5

Powerful Decisions

Every Day Is Judgment Day

As leaders, we are paid for our judgment. A decision is the result of this judgment. If we make better decisions faster, we get better results faster. When Julius Caesar decided to cross the River Rubicon, it set in motion a chain of events that eventually led to his ascension to ultimate power in the Roman Empire. On the other hand, history is full of poor decision making by leadership. For example, Borders, once a major bookseller, made the critical mistake of outsourcing its online book sales to Amazon in the early 2000s. This opened the door for Amazon to gain control of the online book market, and Borders never recovered. As online book sales grew, Borders' physical stores struggled, and the company filed for bankruptcy in 2011.

If we want to improve our decision-making prowess, we need to eliminate everything that undermines the quality of our decision-making ability. Our default decision-making mode is no longer enough. In this chapter, we explore the factors that cloud the effectiveness of decision making by leaders.

Expertise Versus Opinion

Since leadership involves complex and opaque issues, our first decision is how to best utilize experts to access external information. An expert is someone who provides additional knowledge and expertise to improve our judgment. For example, an expert in artificial intelligence (AI) will have a superior perspective on the uses and especially the limits of AI.

How do you recognize real expertise? Our first consideration must be how to distinguish pseudo-expert noise from real expert signals to make better decisions. When assessing the validity of any expert, use the following rules:

- Real experts have deep knowledge, which is limited to their particular field. Since it takes time and focus to build this expertise, consider them ignorant outside their field. It's easy to have an opinion; it's much more difficult to have an informed opinion.
- Extraordinary claims from any expert require extraordinary evidence.
- When experts use apocalyptic language ("the world as we know it will end unless …"), they probably want to sell you something.
- If there is consensus among experts about second and third-order effects in complex systems, you're not dealing with wisdom and intelligence but with dogmas and myopic thinking.
- Computer models of complex systems are simulations based on a set of key assumptions. Real experts focus on the validity of these key assumptions, not on the simulation outcomes.
- There is no such thing as a "Futurist."
- All expert predictions of the future are wrong. Some are useful.
- If the same group of experts advocates the same easy solution for every complex problem, this solution is the actual problem.
- Anyone with a consistent track record of being wrong with past predictions is not an expert, but an entertainer.
- The application of advanced mathematics in social science is usually a sign that you are dealing with people who aren't experts in either of these two fields.

The second consideration when relying on an expert is Wittgenstein's ruler: If you use a ruler to measure something, you also need to trust that the ruler itself is accurate. If the ruler is unreliable, then any measurement you take with it will also be unreliable. In the certification industry we have an endless list of certifying bodies, ranging from the Certified Public Accountant (CPA) exam, to Lloyd's Certification Standards for Pressure Vessels. Ask yourself, "Is the certifying body reliable, trustworthy, and do they provide a real stamp of quality?" In other words, "Do they exhibit deep expertise?"

Is certification based on a vast amount of historical data, and does it provide accurate and consistent predictions of future success? If so, certification has value—think accountancy or engineering. Otherwise, certification has little meaning. Many of the popular personality-based certifications, such as Enneagrams, lack historical data and a track record of consistent and predictable results. They operate in the domain of opinion, not expertise. In that case, a much better approach is to use references from peers and testimonials as selection criteria instead. In environments lacking hard data, the greater the emphasis on certification credentials, the more justified the skepticism.

Diversity Versus Conformity

Another important consideration for making better decisions is to be receptive to diverse perspectives. Not long ago, Toyota unveiled an innovative new design for its next-generation hydrogen engine. The response was mixed. There was enthusiasm from hydrogen proponents and skepticism from EV (electric vehicle) advocates. This episode tells us something about the value of diversity.

First, our worldview is shaped by how we filter information. Although we have access to the same data set, diverse views often emerge from the data we choose to ignore (noise) and the data we choose to acknowledge (signal).

Second, diverse perspectives are only useful if they are based on, or connected to, domain-specific knowledge. The opinion of a beekeeper about the safety system design of a nuclear reactor should be ignored. However, the beekeeper may have very useful insights on how urban planners can design the cities of the future.

Third, the value of diversity reaches its maximum when it's used to nurture an ecosystem of singular, independent, and focused entities that have very different belief systems. For example, an ecosystem with 100 independent, yet diverse engineers is much more innovative and robust than an ecosystem consisting of one organization with 100 dependent engineering employees, even if this organization is run by a very diverse leadership team.

The biggest contribution to diversity is to promote leaders who have two things in common: 1) the wisdom to recognize the limits of their own knowledge, and 2) the courage to allow others maximum freedom to operate outside these limits.

Static Versus Moving

In early 2020, the Conference Board published a report on the pressing concerns of global CEOs that included attracting and retaining top talent, recession risks, and digital transformation. But just 2 months later everything changed. COVID-19 was declared a global pandemic, and suddenly, every other concern vanished into obscurity. For the first time in decades, CEOs faced a singular, overwhelming challenge. The pandemic was a tidal wave that swept away all previous priorities.

Humans are wired to focus on movement, to be drawn toward what's changing and urgent. But we are blind to what is static, to what quietly matters the most—until it's too late. This is the Feline Focus Fallacy. We behave like cats, chasing the frantic flickering dot of the laser pointer, while the true dangers lurk unseen in the background.

At the time of writing this book (2024), we face this same trap once again. The current top concerns for CEOs, according to the Conference Board, are recession and inflation, attracting and retaining talent, innovation, and AI. Every one of these concerns speaks to movement—volatile markets, shifting economic forces, and the latest technological trends. But none of them address the deeper, more insidious risks that remain static, the very risks that could unravel everything. The greatest blind spot in leadership decision making isn't what's moving too fast; it's what we think isn't moving at all. Better decision making starts with ignoring the dots and focusing on the foundations.

Signal Versus Noise

The Tamagotchi is one of the more curious phenomena of the 1990s. It was a keychain with a virtual digital pet that had to be nurtured, fed, and played with, otherwise, it would die. Peak Tamagotchi was finally achieved when the toys were forbidden at school because children skipped lessons to feed their pets. We now laugh at the fact that in those days real life was ignored to take care of something like a digital pet. We think ourselves wiser. The Tamagotchi didn't die out, however, but evolved into cell phones, tablets, and smart watches. Instead of digital pets on key-chains, our fixation is now drawn by social media. Their algorithms have become advanced weaponry to manipulate our attention. Since focusing on signal and ignoring noise is the only superpower that we truly con-trol, the lure of the modern Tamagotchi requires that we deploy advanced countermeasures. We need to shore up our defenses to protect our focus. A practical rule to maintain focus on signal is never to allow yourself to be interrupted by something that is not human.

Useful Versus Actionable

How do you deal with information overload when you need to make a decision? An effective solution is to apply a simple filter: Information is only useful when it's relevant to your goals, inspiring, or entertain-ing. Everything else is just noise and should be ignored. However, this approach is now under threat. The amount of data vying for our atten-tion is unlimited, unlike our attention span. We need better separation technology.

Separation technology, a branch of chemical engineering, deals with the partitioning of different substances. For this, we often use filters or membranes. Generally speaking, filters work like a sieve: Separation takes place based on particle size, similar to how sand is separated from water. Membranes, however, not only separate on a much smaller molecular level but often allow two different molecules to travel in opposite direc-tions. For example, a lung membrane allows oxygen to enter and carbon dioxide to exit the bloodstream.

If we want to deal with information overload, it's no longer enough to apply a simple filter. We need to replace it with a membrane.

This means that useful information should not only be relevant to goals but also actionable. This differentiates improving potential—information stored for possible future use, a one-way street—from im-proving performance, which involves quickly transforming information into meaningful action, a two-way street.

It's time for an upgrade: to exchange our information filters for more sophisticated information membranes.

Risk Versus Reward

Would you join a game of Russian roulette, with a billion-dollar prize if you survive? For most of us, this is not a good bet; the risk of losing your life is too heavy a price to pay. On the other hand, as a multimillionaire, would you invest a million dollars in a start-up, with a potential payoff of a billion dollars? This sounds like a much better deal.

The two components that drive this type of decision making are risk versus reward (Figure 5.1).

Our decision-making energy is a limited resource and this matrix helps us to make optimal use of it. Thus, we get the following:

> If the decision exposes you to low risk and a low reward, don't spend any mental energy on this decision. Make the decision by coin flip and move forward. The color scheme of your main building entrance will not make a difference in achieving your strategic goals.

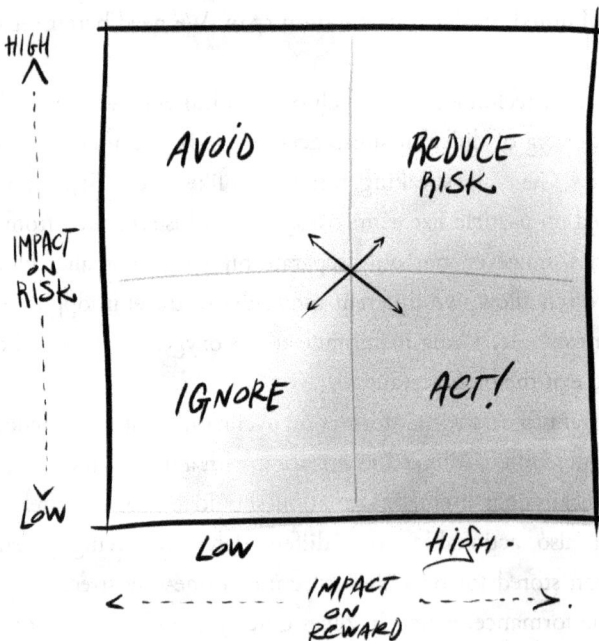

Figure 5.1 *The Smart Decision Grid: how to make better decisions using Risk versus Reward*

If the decision involves high risk and a low reward, avoid it at all costs.

If the decision exposes you to high risk and high reward, focus your mental energy on reducing risk.

There are four ways to mitigate the downside of risk:

- Transfer risk to someone else, which is the core idea behind insurance. Insurance is only necessary when you cannot shoulder the consequences if things go wrong. For example, having legal insurance is a good idea because there is no limit to the cost of legal fees when facing a lawsuit. On the other hand, you may question whether luggage insurance for traveling is necessary. After all, the worst-case scenario has limits—you lose the amount you paid for your luggage and its contents. Insurance should only protect against tail risks—those events which can have a large or even unlimited negative impact. This type of thinking is very relevant to our decision-making process in other areas. Never expose yourself to any scenario where you either face unlimited downside or cannot absorb the worst-case scenario. The key to better decision making is to ignore minor negatives and instead focus obsessively on avoiding ruinous outliers.
- Reduce risk by setting big goals while committing to small investments of time, energy, and money at every step of the way to achieving these goals.
- Eliminate risk completely. For example, in deep-sea drilling, the risk of losing human life can be eliminated by using robots.
- Spread the risk by adopting a portfolio of innovation bets instead of putting all your eggs in one basket.

Finally, if the decision results in a low-risk, high-reward situation, move quickly with everything you have. Too many times, I have seen leaders fretting over small decisions or trying to make a high-risk decision work. Instead, the time is often better spent focusing solely on creating and executing low-risk, high-reward activities.

Uncertainty Versus Risk

Whenever I'm scheduled to do a keynote address overseas, I always plan to arrive at my destination 2 days in advance. It not only helps me adjust to the time difference but also prevents any mishaps due to travel delays. Travel delays may occur because of unexpected events such as overbooked planes, a flat car tire, or an upset stomach. All of these individual occurrences have a low chance of happening. However, the overall probability of a delay is made up of the small probabilities of all individual delays. Since I can think of many reasons that my travel schedule might be delayed, the overall risk to my travel schedule is actually very high. This is a concept called the high probability of low-probability events.

Thus, it's important to make a distinction between risk and uncertainty. My plane not flying has a risk, which is a number based on historical data. Whether or not I will arrive in New York, however, is uncertain. There are a million ways to sabotage my travel, ranging from making a mistake setting the alarm clock to having a flat tire. This means that there is a risk that the plane will not fly, but it's uncertain if I will arrive in New York.

In reality, when organizations talk about risk management, their conception of it only deals with a tiny part of the entire uncertain context. Managing risks is therefore often useless. The key is to manage uncertainty.

The secret to dealing with this phenomenon is to avoid putting too much energy into trying to prevent small probability events. For example, a spare tire in my car will help me mitigate the risk of travel delays caused by a flat tire. Yet it will do nothing to prevent all the other unfortunate events that may cause delays. Instead, choose an option that mitigates overall uncertainty, even if a small probability event happens. In my case, the solution is to add an additional day to my travel schedule. Optionality decreases uncertainty.

Game of Chaos Versus Game of Control

"Do you expect me to talk?" "No, Mr. Bond, I expect you to die."

This is the dialogue between archvillain Auric Goldfinger and James Bond in the movie *Goldfinger*. For context, James Bond is about to be cut in two by a giant laser. Spoiler alert: Our hero manages to live another day.

This intriguing dialogue shows that James Bond thinks he is playing a game of negotiation, with its defined set of rules. What he finds out is that Goldfinger is playing a very different game, which is extermination, with a very different set of rules. In our professional lives, it's important to understand which game we are playing and what the rules are.

In an orderly professional game—think of accountancy, dentistry, or architecture—the rules are clear and transparent. In a Game of Order, rule changes are gradual, with advanced notice. These games are won by the Masters of Consistency. In a chaotic professional game—start-ups, innovation, or high-tech—the rules are opaque and hidden. Rule changes are sudden, without any advance notice. A Game of Chaos is won by the Masters of Adaptability. One of the biggest mistakes we make is succumbing to the Illusion of Control. We convince ourselves that we operate in an orderly professional game, ruled by best practices and a limited set of predictable futures. Too late, we find out that we have been playing a Game of Chaos all along.

Not long ago, a billion Microsoft-operated computers suddenly showed the blue screen of death due to a programming error from an external piece of security software. At that moment, many realized that they had been using the rules of a Game of Order to attempt to control a Game of Chaos. It's futile to try to control a Game of Chaos. It's much more useful to develop options to reduce the negative effects of chaotic events instead.

Path Dependent Versus Path Independent

Imagine two neighbors living in an upscale neighborhood. They're both well off, happy, and retired. One neighbor has been an accountant her entire professional life. The other won the lottery at some point in the past. Now, let's do a thought experiment. Imagine we could restart the lives of both neighbors in a Monte Carlo simulation, thousands of times in a row. The result is that the accountant would end up affluent in the majority of these simulations. The lottery winner, on the other hand, has only one path to achieve her current success: Her achievement is path dependent.

Path dependency is the Achilles heel of many best practices: the drive to adopt processes and systems from other industries to improve. Many best practices are not universal, but specific to an industry, time period, or place. For example, the open office workspace may have been effective in certain organizations dominated by extroverts but is disastrous when introverts are brought into the mix.

A hallmark of excellent best practices is that they have a long and proven record, covering multiple industries. A great example is the extensive use of checklists. Very few new ideas have the power to exceed this high bar. The distinction between a best practice and a lottery ticket is very thin indeed.

Limited Versus Scarce

How do you create a culture that fosters better team decisions when information is scarce rather than limited? The key is to take action anyway. These distinctions will help:

- Speed versus rigor: If a team quickly reaches consensus on a difficult decision, it means they haven't given it enough thought. Reconvene, pursue different perspectives, and discuss the decision again later.
- Final versus flexible: A team decision is final unless new information arises that is relevant to the decision.
- Test versus commitment: A huge commitment, such as building a new factory, requires much more analysis than agreeing to conduct a small test. It's very difficult to change course after a significant commitment. A small test, however, allows you the opportunity to reverse course if needed.
- Reversible versus irreversible: Irreversible means you can't undo the decision—like trying to put toothpaste back into the tube. On the other hand, reversible decisions can be made quickly.
- Options versus constraints: Favor decisions that increase optionality and reduce constraints.

Key Actionable Takeaways

1. **Eliminate Overreliance on Experts**: Stop depending solely on external opinions. Focus on building internal judgment skills to identify true expertise and challenge superficial knowledge.

2. **Stop Chasing Noise Over Signal**: Remove distractions caused by fleeting trends, crises, or irrelevant information. Redirect focus to stable, foundational elements that drive long-term success.

3. **Discard Path-Dependent Strategies**: Avoid plans that rely on a single, unrepeatable success story. Opt for flexible, adaptable solutions that work across various scenarios and industries.

4. **Quit Trying to Control Chaos**: Let go of attempts to dominate chaotic systems with rigid control. Instead, focus on increasing optionality—developing strategies that allow adaptability to unforeseen changes.

5. **End Excessive Risk Mitigation**: Eliminate efforts to address every small risk. Concentrate on preventing catastrophic outcomes while accepting manageable uncertainties.

6. **Avoid Overprocessing Information**: Stop using basic filters that oversimplify data. Adopt dynamic "membrane" thinking to separate relevant, actionable information from static noise.

7. **Minimize Trivial Decision Making**: Remove low-stakes decisions from your focus by delegating or automating them. Reserve mental energy for critical, high-impact choices.

8. **Eliminate Reactive Decision Making**: Stop defaulting to immediate responses triggered by external changes. Prioritize thoughtful, proactive decisions based on broader strategic goals.

9. **Abandon Conformity in Perspective**: Reduce the influence of homogenous thinking by encouraging diverse, domain-relevant perspectives. This helps avoid blind spots in decision making.

10. **Cut Time Wasted on Low-Risk Decisions**: For decisions with low risk and low reward, simplify the process—make quick choices and allocate time to higher-impact issues.

CHAPTER 6

Time Bandits

The Clock Is Ticking

The most important number for any busy leader is 1,440—the number of minutes in a day. Time is your ultimate resource. It's the only relevant resource that is completely out of your control or anyone else's. The reason is that time has two very specific characteristics. First, it cannot be manipulated. You can't stop it, slow it down, or expand it. At the end of the day, those 1,440 minutes are gone forever. Second, it's the only part of the future that behaves in a very consistent, predictable, and reliable way. Its future characteristics are identical to its current and past characteristics. It's linear and unstoppable.

Since the nature of time is a given for all of us, our role is to take full ownership of how we use it. This means that we exchange our time for what we perceive as valuable. Value can have multiple dimensions, such as spending time with our family, reading a good book, or sending people to Mars. With the Michelangelo principle in mind, the question is how to use the time that we have to create the maximum value that we want. In our discussion, we will limit ourselves to answering this question as it pertains to our role as leaders. The personal dimension is, of course, just as important (if not more so). The idea, however, is that the progress we make in our professional lives will have major benefits in our personal lives as well. Just ask the busy executive whose grueling travel schedule prevents her from spending enough quality time with her children.

The simple but profound truth is that the way we organize our day is the way we organize our life. Accomplishing more in the long run requires that we rethink how we use our time in the short run. We need to rethink how to eliminate time bandits which waste our precious time.

All Is Not Well

In my coaching work with accomplished executives, I have come across subtle warning signs that tell me all is not well with how they deal with time.

- A Retirement Countdown Calendar: At the end of the rainbow is the retirement date. On top of the executive's desk, there is a calendar that counts down the days until happiness will finally arrive. Progress is proudly displayed to all visitors to the office. If you're looking forward to retirement, it's often a sign that you're done before you're gone.
- Watchdog at the Gate: Usually, this takes the form of a secretary or personal assistant whose sole task seems to be to limit and delay all access to the busy executive. Instead of being in control, this approach signals desperation.
- Wall to Wall: The executive's schedule is densely packed with meetings and appointments. As a result, appointments start chronically late, feel rushed, and neither end on time nor on a high note.
- Negative Reputation: People and products are known for a maximum of three things. If your reputation contains the words "busy," "late," and "short-tempered," it's time to step back and reflect.
- Humble Bragging: Telling strangers how hard you work within 2 minutes of first contact is a subtle form of showing off. Sometimes, it even hides a lack of actual accomplishment.

Increasing accomplishments requires that you use the time to focus on what really matters. This is the difference between movement and achievement.

What Really Matters

Let me introduce the concept of the highest and best use of time. These activities all have three characteristics:

1. You're skilled at the activity: I define skill as the ability to consistently perform a complex task with a positive outcome. Examples

of these activities are project management, professional speaking, influencing others, advanced mathematics, or setting strategy.

2. You're passionate about the activity: Passion means that there is no resistance to starting, you maintain high energy while being engaged, and you continue until finished. Work doesn't feel like work but feels like play.

3. You're creating value for other people: Value means that other people are willing to invest resources to obtain the results of your work. The most common way of investing is with money.

The concept of the highest and best use of time is represented by the intersection between skills, passion, and value. I call this the Golden Triangle (Figure 6.1).

Consider what happens when one of these three elements is missing.

- If skill is missing, you operate like an amateur. Your intentions may be good, but the results are clearly lacking.
- If passion is missing, you're an automaton, going through the motions. The technical term for this state of mind is simply having a job. Work feels like work.

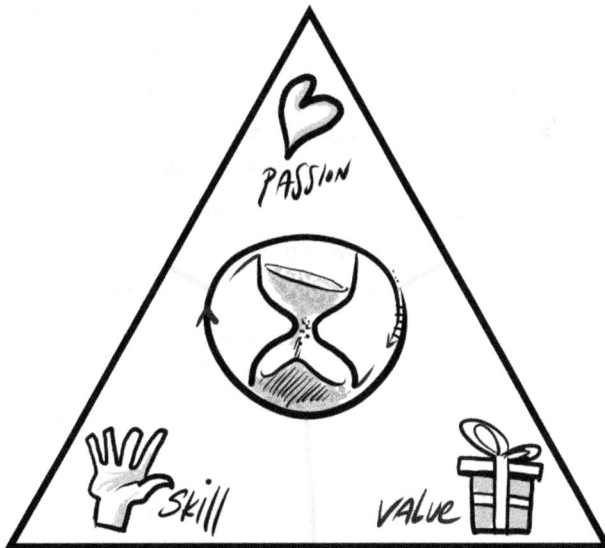

Figure 6.1 The Golden Triangle: how to determine your highest and best use of time

- If value creation for others is missing, you have a hobby—
  spending time for your own benefit. This is important to lead a
  satisfying and balanced life, yet it will not advance your professional accomplishments.

To engage in the highest and best use of time is, therefore, straightforward: Understand what is not your highest and best use of time. Next, get
rid of it. For this, we need to get a better understanding of our own skills,
passions, and value creation.

Become Skilled at Recognizing Skills

An example of a skill every leader should possess is high-performance
judgment. It's the ability to make better decisions under uncertainty.
This skill can be applied in different areas of executive interest. A marketing executive may apply high-performance judgment to design and
execute a new product launch strategy. An operations executive might
use high-performance judgment to set up a critical safety review process
for a new chemical plant. A leader of a legal department may exercise
high-performance judgment for risk assessment.

High-performance judgment is based on a mix of skills. The marketing
executive is effective because of a combination of process thinking, influencing stakeholders, public speaking, external orientation, resilience in the
face of obstacles, and the like. Applying these skills in concert is second nature for effective leaders. Breaking the individual skills down is, therefore,
not an easy task. Yet it is important, since understanding your skills enables you to systematically improve. For example, if you don't know why
you're so proficient at hiring talent, you won't be able to repeat the process.

An effective way to understand your skills is to make them transfer-
able to others. Imagine you want to teach a 3-day course about your role
in the organization. How would you set up the elements of this course?

The Passion of the Executive

Which activities would you continue to do, even if you were the last
human on Earth?

Funktionslust is a German term that refers to the pleasure you get simply from engaging in a certain activity. Dogs love to chase Frisbees, birds enjoy swooping down from the sky, and horses will run fast whenever they have the opportunity.

This is also true for humans: Painters love to paint, writers live to write, and divers want to dive. Each of these activities is a pleasure in and of itself and is not necessarily connected to an actual end goal, purpose, or serving others. Accomplished leaders are sometimes so goal-obsessed that they forget about the pleasure of doing the activity itself. This is a major source of anxiety and stress: We're always busy chasing the next milestone without enjoying the process of getting there.

Therefore, the interesting question is not to ask yourself what you're uniquely designed to achieve in this world but to ask yourself what you're uniquely designed to do in this world. The answer to this question is the core of your passion.

Myths About Creating Value

How do you improve the condition of others and increase value? A sales executive not only improves the condition of her organization by increasing the bottom line but also allows potential clients to reap the benefits of the products or services being sold.

There are three persistent myths around creating value:

1. The Hourly Rate Myth: The value we create is determined by the amount of time we have used, not by how we have used the time. This fallacy is the reason that many employees, contractors, and consultants are still paid by the hour. This implies that value creation is time-based and independent of efficiency and effectiveness.
2. The Giant Sacrifice Myth: The importance and quality of a project are determined by the amount of effort we have used to complete the project. The fact that a PhD student has worked hard and put in enormous investment of 4 years of their life into conducting research does not necessarily mean it's good or useful research.
3. The Entitlement Myth: Seniority is based on the amount of time someone has spent in the same job. This mentality assumes that

repetitive and long experience provides insight, judgment, and value creation. Instead, intelligence, creativity, and cross-functional experience are often more important drivers of high performance, especially for leaders.

Therefore, all value that is based on time spent, effort invested, or experience gained is imaginary. Spending more hours, putting in more effort, or gaining more experience may not be the highest and best use of your time as a leader.

Avoiding Fake Jobs

Recently, after a long flight, I was surprised to go through five (!) immigration checks, all doing the same thing—checking my passport. I realized this meant that either the work of an immigration officer is so sloppy that additional quality controls are necessary, or four of these five officers had fake jobs.

What's a fake job? It's an organizational role that does not contribute to the strategic goals of the organization and does not create value. To identify these, we need to understand how a job can add value.

It can:

- Create future value: Think of innovation or R&D activities.
- Create current value: Take, for example, lean Six Sigma optimization, operations, or sales.
- Prevent value destruction: Examples are quality control or audits.
- Release value: This includes marketing or creating a successful environment for high-performance teams.
- Distribute value: Take, for example, financial activities such as budgeting.

A fake job will either:

- Consume value: Resources are used without making tangible progress toward the strategic goals of the organization.

- Destroy value: Resources are used with negative progress toward the strategic goals of the organization. Considering its lousy track record, mergers and acquisitions are a notorious example of value killers.

The tricky part is that some people might be really good at these unnecessary jobs. In the hilarious movie *Galaxy Quest*, Sigourney Weaver plays a starship crew member who knows she has a fake job; she would repeat any spoken message from the starship's computer to the bridge crew verbatim. When confronted with this inconvenient fact, she sighs: "It may be a fake job, but I'm very good at it."

If you want to understand exactly how you create value for others, ask yourself the following: If I were to win the lottery today and find myself tomorrow sipping cocktails on the beach in the Bahamas:

- What would go wrong at my company in the short term?
- What would go wrong at my company in the long term?
- Who would be negatively affected or even devastated?

With everything else, your contribution may be redundant, replaceable, or irrelevant.

Applying the Golden Triangle

The Golden Triangle can be used in two specific ways. One, it provides immediate clarity about how to best use your time, the time of your team, and the time of your organization. Two, it provides a roadmap for your personal, team, and organizational strategic development goals.

Let's take a close look at your current highest and best use of time. Doing more of the activities in your Golden Triangle requires that you first quit the activities that are not in your Golden Triangle. The reason is that your most important resource, time, is fixed. Therefore doing more of something requires that you do less of something else. I call this approach strategic quitting: You have to let go in order to reach out.

We have discussed earlier that all activities where you have limited skill, lack passion, and do not create much value are prime candidates for strategic quitting. If you want to systematically identify these activities, ask yourself, "Knowing what I know now, which of the activities I'm currently engaged in would I choose not to even start if I could do it all over again?" This approach is called zero-based thinking.

Typical areas to consider are:

- Processes and systems, such as HR onboarding and talent management.
- Clients, especially toxic clients who drain much of your energy and don't add much value anyway.
- Vendors who don't stick to agreements, are difficult, and require much hand-holding.
- Team members who decrease the energy level of others and require a lot of cleaning up after.
- Projects that are stuck and won't deliver the envisioned result.
- Products and services that are loss leaders and don't have a bright future.
- Markets that don't show any promise or growth.
- Technology that's not working.
- Add-ons to products and services that are not even currently valued by your clients.
- Data collection that is not turned into actionable insights.

A recent crisis or setback provides interesting opportunities to apply zero-based thinking. Which of your clients, vendors, and team members were operating "above the line" when times were tough? Who was there for you, operated as a partner, and went the extra mile to help you out? Next, who operated "below the line?" They were inflexible, unyielding, and stressed the formal part of the relationship. Once you have made both lists, determine a strategy to strategically quit those clients, vendors, and team members who operated below the line. After all, it's in times of crisis that you need to be surrounded by people who love the work.

A fun way to engage your team in zero-based thinking is an exercise called "Lights On, Now What?" In this exercise, you pretend that you and your management team have just bought the company. It's your first day. You don't have any obligations, only big dreams and wild ambitions. How would you set up the organization from scratch? This exercise will provide you with new and surprising insights into all the areas where strategic quitting can be applied with gusto.

Recently, I spoke to an accomplished surgeon. She mentioned that her Golden Triangle consists of three activities:

1. Diagnosing a patient.
2. Performing surgery.
3. Evaluating the effectiveness of the intervention.

This is why surgeons do not clean operating rooms, iron the hospital linens, or cook meals for their patients. If you see your work as equivalent to that of a surgeon, why are you still cleaning, ironing, or cooking?

The point of the highest and best use of your time is often clear for many leaders. So, why is strategic quitting still tough to do?

The MINI and the Momentum

A body in motion at a constant velocity will remain in motion unless acted upon by an outside force. This is Newton's First Law of Motion. What's true for objects is true for humans and organizations as well. We continue an activity unless an outside force, such as a deliberate decision, stops us. Motion is hard to break, and this often leads to inefficiencies, waste, and even disaster. I call this the Momentum Fallacy.

Take, for example, the MINI. When automotive engineers developed the MINI in the 1950s, an important design consideration was low cost. To paint the car, the chassis was held in the air by a pole that protruded from the back to the front of the car. This pole left a hole in the middle of the dashboard. The design engineers were classical pragmatists and decided to use this hole to fit the instrument panel. As such, the iconic design feature of having an instrument panel between the driver and passenger instead of in front of the driver was born. Though this setup was arguably inferior to having all of the instruments placed in front of the driver, it has been enthusiastically copied in many other modern vehicles despite the fact that current technologies have rendered the pole-painting technique obsolete. This inefficiency has now become part of accepted automobile design.

A practical way to overcome the Momentum Fallacy is to use a sunset clause: Any new rule, initiative, or activity will automatically be abandoned after a certain specified time unless a new and deliberate decision is made to continue. Permanence is the most dangerous illusion of time. This is why systematically thinking about strategic quitting is such a powerful tool to accelerate performance.

Become a Strategic Quitter

Once you have identified all of the areas that are not your David as described in the Michelangelo Principle, there are five ways you can begin to apply strategic quitting.

Elimination

The worst use of your time is not doing things inefficiently but doing things that shouldn't be done in the first place—in other words, becoming excellent at something irrelevant. For example, improving your proofreading skills for client proposals to look for grammatical errors is rapidly becoming an irrelevant skill in the era of AI.

Recently, I worked with a group of senior finance professionals at a large oil company on strategic quitting. We quickly concluded that the biggest opportunity to apply the Michelangelo Principle was in reporting. A lot of departmental time was spent preparing financial reports. Many of these reports were commissioned in the distant past, and since the world had changed they were no longer relevant in the current business environment. The team quickly decided on a shortlist of potential reports that could be eliminated. But to acknowledge that discontinuing the reports could prove sensitive—it's human nature to become defensive when changing things—they decided to send out the next batch of reports digitally, with a twist. For security reasons, all reports were password protected. In the accompanying e-mail, it was made clear that the password to open the report could be retrieved by personal request to the finance department. Then they waited 6 weeks and eliminated every report that didn't have any password requests.

Delegation

Often, delegation is defined as giving work to someone else. I prefer a different definition. For me, delegation means giving something that feels like work for you to someone for whom it feels like play.

When leading a team of engineers, one of my responsibilities was to organize and execute the management of the change process in our operations facility. This is a very important process, but because of its repetitiveness, I got easily bored. However, in my team, there was a skilled engineer who loved owning and executing this process. Delegation was done quickly. She would run the management of the change process within the parameters we both had agreed upon beforehand. In exchange, I would do part of her work, which was data analysis, something I loved.

This is the essence of high-performing teams: Together, they do what must be done as a team, but individually, they work on those things that are their highest and best use of their time. High performance is about a relentless focus on building on your strengths. It's much easier to become twice as good at the things you are already good at than to marginally improve the things you are very bad at. In other words, if you focus your entire life on trying to compensate for your weaknesses instead of building on your strengths, you will end up with a large set of strong weaknesses. This is not a recipe for great accomplishments.

Think of your performance management systems. Are they geared toward building on strengths or compensating for weaknesses?

Outsourcing

This is the core of modern business. Every client has outsourced a specific part of their value creation process to you. The reason is that you can do it more efficiently, with more passion, and often with a better result. When should you outsource an activity? When doing the activity requires time that can be better used to create more value.

Another way of outsourcing is to have the task performed by a system or a process. An example is having an excellent Customer Relationship Management (CRM) system to replace a lot of clumsy manual work in an Excel database.

Optimization

If a task is not part of your Golden Triangle and cannot be eliminated, delegated, or outsourced, an option is to optimize it. What can you do to achieve the result in the laziest way possible? When taking over a business intelligence team, we had about 20 boxes of material that had to be reviewed and archived. Since we were the experts, this was something we had to do. So, we decided to make it a game. We named every box after a Disney character. Every day, we chose a random character and quickly reviewed the box associated with that character. We had fun, and the task was completed within a month.

Postponing

The last approach to strategic quitting is to put a project or initiative on hold. For this, it's helpful to create a "someday/maybe" list with all initiatives that are dormant but can be activated in the future. Two things are important. First, review this list regularly, say once every 3 months. Second, be very clear in your communication that no energy should be put into any of the projects or activities on this list. Otherwise, an organization continues to work on them. I call this a Zombie List—everything that has been formally canceled but is still alive and consuming resources.

Strategic quitting is the core activity of every high-performance leader. "More–better–faster" is for amateurs. Professionals have mastered the art of strategic quitting.

The Need for Strategic Sacrifice

Your current Golden Triangle may not be your future Golden Triangle. Think of your Golden Triangle from, say, 10 years ago. It was probably very different from your current Golden Triangle. Several factors may have caused this shift, such as evolving technology, shifting interests, or a different marketplace.

Consider cardiothoracic surgery which deals with operating on the heart and lungs. Surgeons have performed these complex operations for more than 50 years. The results are phenomenal: very high patient recovery rates with very low mortality risks. The surgeons are true masters of their craft. Highly complicated operations are successfully performed with great precision and routine. Because of these impressive results, it also means that the field of cardiothoracic surgery runs the risk of stagnation. In highly successful environments, new ideas to do things differently are often met with resistance and skepticism. There is incremental improvement, but what about real innovation? Why change what works and works well?

True mastery and high performance imply the ability to consistently and effectively achieve a complex, almost magical result, and the courage to reinvent yourself to take your current expertise to the next level.

To make this shift, it's not enough to apply strategic quitting to get rid of everything that is not part of your current Golden Triangle. You also need to imagine your future Golden Triangle. In order to move to this future, it's necessary to let go of activities that are currently not your highest and best use of time (Figure 6.2).

For an IT executive, it may mean stopping solving complex problems and teaching others to solve them instead. For a sales executive, it could mean handing over personal relationships with your best customers to other sales team members so that you can develop new relationships with your future best clients.

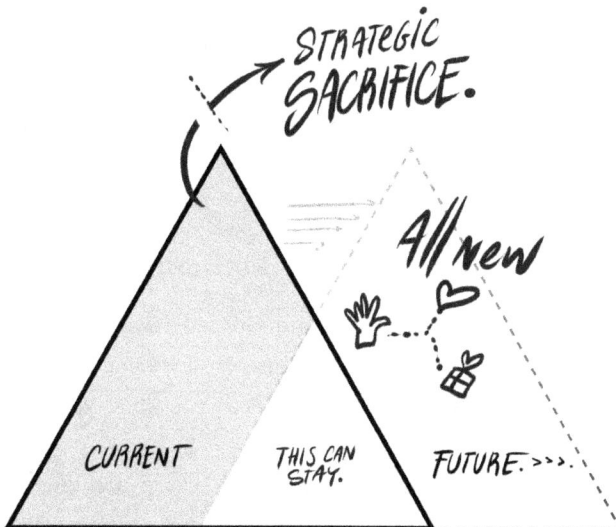

Figure 6.2 Strategic Sacrifice: how to shift value creation in time

To identify your future Golden Triangle, ask yourself:

- Which new skills do I need to develop for my future, 3 years from now?
- What experiments do I need to conduct to identify the next level of my passion?
- What significant value can I create for my future clients with my new skillsets and passion?

Movement Versus Achievement

Being in motion and taking fast action can have downsides. When I ask my clients how they're doing, the default response is often "busy." This makes me curious: Is it good busy or bad busy? There's a difference between movement and achievement. Movement is about doing things, exhibiting type A behavior, and taking action for action's sake. Achievement is about consistently making progress toward your most important goals. Or, in Michelangelo terms: Busy is about hammering away at the marble, while achievement is about releasing the David. Two very different things.

Extraordinary productivity means making maximum progress toward your most important goals within the time you choose to spend. You can be extraordinarily productive working 20, 40, or 60 hours a week. However, if you decide to work 60 hours, you should accomplish three times more than you do in 20 hours. Spending 60 hours doing what could be done in 20 is a giant waste of your time. The Golden Triangle ensures that you stay out of the busy trap.

Key Actionable Takeaways

1. **Eliminate Activities Outside Your Golden Triangle**: Remove tasks that do not align with your skills, passions, or value creation. Freeing this time allows you to focus on activities where you excel and create the most impact.
2. **Cut Nonessential Meetings and Reports**: Stop attending or producing meetings and reports that do not generate actionable insights or add clear value. For example, use methods like

password-protected reports to test their relevance—eliminate those that receive no requests.

3. **Stop Supporting "Fake Jobs"**: Identify roles or activities that consume resources without contributing to strategic goals. Remove or reallocate these to ensure all efforts create tangible value.

4. **Remove the Momentum Fallacy**: Avoid continuing activities simply because they've always been done. Apply deliberate decisions to stop tasks that no longer serve your strategic direction.

5. **Discard "Zombie" Projects**: Formally end initiatives that have been canceled but still consume resources. Regularly review a "Zombie List" to ensure such tasks are fully eliminated.

6. **End Activities Tied to Outdated Goals**: Use zero-based thinking to ask: "If I weren't already doing this, would I start it today?" Eliminate projects and tasks that fail this test to refocus efforts on relevant priorities.

7. **Stop Resisting Strategic Sacrifices**: Let go of even high-performing tasks that no longer align with your evolving goals or future vision. Strategic quitting allows room for reinvention and new opportunities.

8. **Cease Adding Layers to Solve Complexity**: Avoid counterproductive fixes like extra processes or staff to combat inefficiency. Instead, eliminate the root causes of complexity to streamline systems.

9. **Avoid Overoptimizing Low-Value Tasks**: Don't waste time improving tasks that shouldn't be done at all. Focus optimization efforts only on essential activities that directly support your goals.

10. **Stop Doing What Feels Like Work for You**: Delegate tasks that you find tedious to team members who enjoy them. This aligns responsibilities with strengths and increases team efficiency.

CHAPTER 7

Speed Traps

Speed Matters

Mario Andretti, the accomplished Formula One driver, once said, "If you think you're in control, you're probably not going fast enough." Control and speed are usually mutually exclusive, and sacrificing some measure of control is often necessary to go faster. On the other hand, when we impose needless control, burdening our team with unnecessary rules that add to their workload, for example, we reduce speed.

In the thirteenth century, the Mongols, led by Genghis Khan, covered vast distances at extraordinary speed. They mastered the use of their cavalry, and their riders moved faster than their enemies could mobilize, which allowed them to strike unexpectedly and retreat before counterattacks could be mounted. The Mongols eliminated everything that slowed them down: They didn't build fortifications, use vast supply trains, or wear heavy armor.

In business, the power of speed is often underestimated. Strategies frequently have a multiyear horizon, and strategic projects can last many months.

A company I once worked for prioritized its safety performance as a key strategic driver of its business. It made vast improvements, first by addressing technical safety issues, then by improving processes and systems. Eventually, however, improvements in safety statistics stalled or even deteriorated. Adding more processes and systems seemed to have the opposite effect, so we decided to change course and focus on speed and simplicity with the identification of 10 lifesaving rules. These were introduced quickly, and as a result, they became the focus of the entire organization. This shift provided a breakthrough in safety performance.

By giving up some control—refusing to add more processes and instead focusing on speed and simplicity—we actually gained more control in the area of safety.

There are two key lessons here. At a certain point, steadily increasing the amount of supposedly good things can lose effectiveness, or can have a negative effect. Exercise is healthy, but too much exercise will exhaust the body, slow you down, and diminish performance. Furthermore, if a once-successful activity starts to show diminishing returns, it's time to quickly shift gears and refocus.

This chapter will therefore focus on identifying and eliminating the most common detours that reduce the speed of you, your team, and your organization.

Meetings Versus Gatherings

Meetings are both a blessing and a curse. Nothing gets done without meetings. Nothing gets done because of meetings. Why do organizations have meetings in the first place? The answer is that substantial goals require substantial collaboration. Typically, when a new leader enters an existing organization, its meeting structure is already well established. Meeting structures are longstanding—the way things have always been done. It's very rare that they're systematically reviewed, challenged, or changed unless there's a significant crisis or a significant opportunity. A fixed meeting structure can quickly get out of sync with the reality of the evolving outside world.

Since meetings are so important, how would you rate the quality of your meetings? In my experience, I have rarely attended a meeting that didn't have room for improvement. On second thought, most of them were horribly bad. They resembled sluggish gatherings instead of dynamic and high-performance summits. If this is the case for you and your team, there is a great opportunity to raise the bar. A vast body of work is already available to help create effective meetings. Here, I will separate the good from the essential for leaders.

There are three areas that drive meeting excellence: objectives, outcomes, and choreography.

Meeting Objectives

A productive meeting can only have three objectives:

- **To make a decision.** Needless to say, effective meetings focus solely on important decisions, not on trivial matters. Signs of a bad meeting culture are either making no decisions or making too many decisions. If nothing is decided, why have the meeting in the first place? If too many things are decided, the agenda is probably loaded with unimportant items.
- **To brainstorm ideas.** Multiple and diverse perspectives catalyze ideas and accelerate thinking. Using a team meeting to generate fresh approaches on new topics is an excellent use of time. Keep in mind that brainstorming is an art in and of itself: There are many poor ways and few good ways to effectively engage a group of people.
- **To drive project progress.** Since projects usually involve multiple people in multiple departments trying to achieve multiple goals, ensuring alignment is critical. A project must be clarified, reviewed, and aligned regularly, and a meeting is an excellent way to achieve this. A progress meeting often combines brainstorming and decision making.

A meeting can cover multiple subjects. In such cases, both the objectives and the sequence of the subjects are important. For each subject, be clear about the objective beforehand. Meetings often get derailed due to misalignment and confusion. Part of the team thinks a subject is on the agenda to share information, another part thinks it's there to generate ideas, while other team members expect decisions to be made or don't think at all.

The sequence of subjects is also crucial. Always start with the most difficult and important subject. Once this is covered, the rest of the meeting will proceed more smoothly and effectively. This approach is known as "putting the dead rat on the table." Any other objectives can likely be achieved by avenues other than a meeting. For example, if basic information needs to be shared, it should be distributed prior to the meeting. The meeting itself can then be used to clarify items, brainstorm ideas, or make decisions. Also, just because the team is meeting doesn't mean you should use the time to check in or do team building. It's better to do those at lunch instead.

Meeting Outcomes

If a meeting doesn't have a clear end goal, you shouldn't have a meeting in the first place. That said, the takeaway of any meeting consists of three parts:

- **Action list.** This contains all agreed-upon actions, the owner responsible for each action, and a date for completion. Only meeting participants can become the owner of an action.
- **Decision list.** This list records all decisions made during the meeting. It ensures clarity and prevents repeated discussions. A decision should only be revisited when new information is available. Another important point is that if a team quickly reaches consensus on a complicated and important subject, it likely hasn't given it enough thought. In such cases, table the subject for the next meeting.
- **Communication list.** No meeting operates in isolation. There will be people not in attendance who need to know about the decisions made or actions committed to. This list ensures these individuals are kept informed. This also means you can eliminate meeting minutes or summaries. Unless needed for legal purposes, they don't serve a significant function. If necessary, you can always record the meeting verbatim and use AI to generate a summary.

Meeting Choreography

Perhaps we can describe a meeting as the subtle dance of focused minds. Perhaps we shouldn't. Regardless, the dance metaphor can help you think like the choreographer of a Broadway musical to create a great performance with these three meeting rules:

- **No preparation, no seat on the table.** When people arrive unprepared, they typically ask for additional reading time, a quick run-through of the presentation, or an executive summary. All of this is a waste of time for those who did prepare. Don't allow it—ever.

- **No agenda, no meeting**. If there is no agenda outlining the subjects to be discussed, the meeting should be canceled. Unclear goals lead to confusing and inefficient meetings.

- **Break Parkinson's Law**. Parkinson's Law states that a task will take as long as the time allocated to it. For instance, if we schedule a meeting for 1 hour, we will meet for the full hour, even if the objective is achieved in 10 minutes. The practical application of this principle is to simply cut the meeting time of your regular meetings in half. First, it will save you a significant amount of time. Second, your meetings will be high-energy and highly effective.

Leaders should drive a great meeting culture. Are your meetings the best in the entire organization? Meetings can either drag down performance or act as a catalyst for achieving great things. Simply put, don't allow bad meeting standards to creep into your organization's culture. Your goal should be to never tolerate bad meetings.

Executive Versus Worker

We all have two different personalities: the Executive and the Worker. The Executive is in charge of thinking: what to do, when to do it, and why it's important. The Executive makes the plans. The Worker is in charge of doing the actual work. The Worker makes it happen. At the start of each day, we are full of energy and the Executive shines: It plans, takes charge, and creates a vision. Afterward, it hands the tasks over to the Worker. But as the day progresses and things need to get done, the Worker runs out of steam. Thinking is hard, and small tasks that require even a little effort start to look difficult. The Worker slowly gives in to the temptation of procrastination.

To overcome procrastination and drive personal productivity, the Executive has to define tasks for the Worker in such a way that the Worker no longer has to think. The Worker should only have to do simple, clearly defined tasks like calling a number, sending a document, or shopping online for an item. To massively improve productivity, we need a system that allows the Executive to set direction and the Worker to drive speed.

This system is called the execution engine.

Building an Execution Engine

Your execution engine consists of two parts: a tangible part and an intangible part.

The tangible part contains the following:

- Goal list. This is an overview of clearly defined goals. (Refer to the chapter on clarity for more details.)
- Project list. A project requires two or more steps to achieve a desired outcome. Setting up a performance review system is a project. Having lunch is not. It's also important to redefine all "blob" projects. In the 1958 movie *The Blob*, an amoeba-like alien life form sets out to absorb and destroy the inhabitants of a small Pennsylvania village. Though fictional, I have encountered many "blobs" in my professional career. A "blob" is a prominent yet unclear initiative with an undefined scope that dominates the focus and conversation of many leaders and employees. It usually involves buzzwords like Quality, Digital, Sustainability, Customer Centricity, or Diversity. If you encounter a blob initiative, your focus should be to help the organization unblob the project. Three key questions will help you become an effective "unblobber":
  1. Scope: What does success look like for this initiative?
  2. Measures of success: How will we know we've achieved success?
  3. Final result: What does "done" look like? Your ability to unblob a project is a secret superpower that can help any organization get unstuck.
- Action list. This is an overview of all physical actions you're committed to in order to make progress on your goals. These actions

can be for others or yourself. A good action list should only contain physical tasks defined in the clearest, smallest, and simplest way possible—tasks your Worker can do mindlessly, without needing to think.

- Someday/Maybe list. This is a list of ideas or projects that might be interesting but you're not yet committed to.
- Waiting-for list. This tracks all requests and actions important to you that have been delegated to others.

The nontangible part of your execution engine contains the high-performance habits that fuel your productivity. In 1998, the British Olympic rowing team realized they were in trouble. Though competent and skilled, they hadn't won any significant events. So, they decided to radically change their approach. They agreed that from that moment until the Olympics, every decision would be preceded by a simple question: Will it make the boat go faster? They soon realized their days were filled with thousands of small decisions. The vast majority of which were subconscious and made on autopilot: what to eat, where to go, how to start the day. However, many of these seemingly tiny decisions mattered when aiming to achieve Olympian performance standards. Gradually, these decisions added up, and the boat began to go faster and faster. Two years later, they won Olympic gold.

By consciously eliminating neutral or bad habits, we create space for positive habits, becoming more efficient and effective in the process. Much has been written about efficiency, time management, and productivity. My focus here is to drill down on the essential habits for busy leaders—the vital few that truly accelerate speed.

But first, I need to address the 5 a.m. myth. The 5 a.m. club is a group of performance enthusiasts who aim to use early mornings to get the most out of their day. I'm not part of this club. I'm most productive when waking up around 6 a.m. It would be nonsensical for me to wake up earlier. A common misconception about high performance is that success is only achieved through huge sacrifices, involving almost draconian standards—such as strict diets, intensive exercise regimens, or deep meditation practices. However, I've found the opposite to be true: You don't need to train for a triathlon to maintain excellent physical health. High performance is about building small, consistent routines that make the most sense for you. Striving for impossible behavioral standards often serves as a convenient excuse to overlook the small, consistent efforts that truly make a difference in life.

Becoming a Productivity Powerhouse

The following high-performance habits will immediately and significantly boost your productivity.

Your Inbox is Not Your Action List

Your action list is derived from your projects, which are based on your goals. Your goals are based on your vision and the vision of your organization. Time spent on your e-mail is only productive if it moves you toward your strategic goals. The job description of an executive—or any professional, for that matter—does not include managing e-mail; it's to create value.

Signs of dysfunction in organizations where e-mail management takes precedence over achieving results include:

- Long and expanding e-mail chains.
- Slow response times to e-mails.
- Fear of using the phone.
- Full inboxes.
- Large CC fields.

The 2-Minute Rule

If an action takes 2 minutes or less, do it now. There are two reasons for this. First, it takes a lot of mental energy to store a reminder and retrieve it later. Second, a 2-minute action usually takes even less than 2 minutes. The practical application for e-mail management is to only touch an e-mail once. Upon reading an e-mail (or any other input), choose from the following options:

- Do it (if it takes less than 2 minutes).
- Delete it (if it doesn't help you achieve your strategic goals).

- Defer it (put it on an action list to handle later).
- Archive it (for future reference).

Your objective should be to work from an empty inbox.

Use Your Golden Hour

One of the most powerful concepts in human productivity is the Golden Hour: the time of day when your mind is at peak performance. During this time, you're more creative, productive, and energetic. The exact timing of the Golden Hour varies from person to person. Mine is between 7.30 and 10 a.m. You can identify your Golden Hour by noticing when you naturally solve difficult problems or engage in creative thinking. Additionally, coworkers might use this time to seek your advice because they subconsciously know you're at your best. Use this precious time to do creative work and deep thinking. Don't waste it on tedious activities or attending unimportant meetings. Instead, plan your day in advance to make the most of these high-performance windows. How can you determine your Golden Hour? Keep a journal. After a few weeks, your Golden Hour will become apparent. Also, ask your coworkers: When do they typically approach you for quality input and deep insights? More importantly, when do they avoid you like the plague?

Apply Task-to-Time

Predefine the amount of time you'll spend on a task. When the time is up, wrap up the task, finish, and ship the outcome. This is the opposite of Parkinson's Law. By forcing ourselves to complete a task within a limited time, we avoid the pitfall of gilding the lily: making something better that is already good enough. Your job is about success, not perfection.

Use the Swiss Cheese Technique

Complete a series of small tasks to slowly poke holes in a larger project. We tend to overestimate what we can accomplish in a day but underestimate what we can achieve in a year. The trick is to consistently work on small tasks that contribute to a big project.

Apply the Productivity Trident

This powerful technique helps maintain momentum and systematic progress on your most important tasks. Define the three most important tasks for the next day. Execute them, regardless of circumstances. Rinse and repeat.

Eat Your Frog

Imagine starting every single day by swallowing a live frog. It's probably the worst thing you'll do all day, so the rest of the day will be easier. The good news is that this is a metaphor: Start your day with the task you dread the most. This will have two benefits: The rest of your day will be highly productive, and it's often the "frog" that holds you back from taking the next step to cross the Valley of Death.

Eat the frog first thing in the morning to maximize your energy benefits throughout the day. Also, don't stare at the frog. If you do, it will only grow bigger and more terrifying.

Avoid the Bike Shed Fallacy

The bike shed fallacy of management attention tells us that if a management team's agenda consists of two items—the color of the new office bike shed and the engineering details of the new nuclear energy plant—most of the discussion will focus on the color of the bike shed.

This behavior can be explained by two thinking patterns. First, thinking is an energy-consuming activity, so we tend to avoid thinking about brain-taxing subjects. Second, it's easier to have an opinion (e.g., "red looks nicer") than an informed opinion (e.g., "there's a mistake in the safety valve calculations"). To avoid wasting time on trivial matters while ignoring essential ones, apply the following approach: Start every meeting with the most important subject and only move on once a decision has been made.

Controlled Access

Your productivity and performance are determined by your ability to maintain focus on your tasks. This requires a system that gives you control over interruptions from other people. Here are three strategies for effective access control:

- Get rid of the "Open Door Policy": Continual open-door policies encourage unintended disruptions. Instead, set designated times for team members to present questions and discussions. This structured approach not only maximizes focus but also encourages a problem-solving mentality among team members, fostering independence and critical thinking.
- Define Emergency Communication Protocols: For situations that require immediate attention, designate a specific communication method as the emergency channel. For example, in my case, clients know that they can send me a text message to get a quick response.
- Be precise and accountable about any time agreements: I make sure that I call at the exact time of any appointment. This behavior creates trust and establishes a reputation for dependability.

Your most precious asset is your time. Put it inside a vault. Then guard the keys like a hawk.

Key Actionable Takeaways

1. **Eliminate Unnecessary Meeting Objectives**: Avoid meetings without clear outcomes. Cancel those with vague agendas or undefined purposes to streamline organizational time and focus.
2. **Stop Supporting Bloated Projects**: Identify and "unblob" large, ambiguous initiatives by clearly defining their scope, success metrics, and desired outcomes. Remove confusion to accelerate progress.
3. **Reduce Cognitive Load in Tasks**: Avoid assigning vague or complex tasks. Break them into simple, actionable steps that require minimal mental effort for rapid execution.

4. **Abandon the Open-Door Policy**: Eliminate constant access interruptions by structuring specific communication windows. Encourage team autonomy and reduce distractions.

5. **Cut Lengthy Meeting Durations**: Challenge the default meeting times. Halve durations to minimize inefficiency, following Parkinson's Law to make meetings more concise and productive.

6. **Discard Legacy Processes**: Question long-standing systems and meetings. Remove outdated structures that no longer serve organizational speed or relevance.

7. **Stop Chasing Perfection in Execution**: Avoid gilding the lily on tasks. Use techniques like predefined time limits or the Swiss Cheese method to maintain momentum and prevent overrefinement.

8. **Minimize Trivial Decision Making**: Eliminate minor, low-impact choices from the agenda. Focus decision-making energy exclusively on high-impact, strategic issues.

9. **End Reactive Task Management**: Avoid using your inbox as an action list. Create a separate system tied to strategic goals for more focused task execution.

10. **Remove Barriers to Peak Productivity**: Guard your Golden Hour fiercely by eliminating interruptions and low-priority tasks during your most productive time of day.

CHAPTER 8

Activating Teams

Welcome to the Valley of Death

Exceptional ambitions require high-performance teams. The marathon is the highlight of any Olympic Games. It's almost a miracle that the majority of runners even reach the finish line. However, if we look at the small minority who don't, something interesting tends to happen at the 18 to 20 mile mark (29–32 km). This moment is often referred to as the Wall. It's the most common point at which runners struggle, and more than 50 percent of all dropouts occur. The physical explanation is that, at this distance, the body's primary fuel source—glycogen—is depleted. Yet the dropout rate does not increase after this point; in fact, it actually decreases and reduces to almost zero the closer an athlete gets to the finish line. This suggests that there is also a mental element at play—after making it past the Wall, the finish line seems to pull athletes in.

In business, the Wall's equivalent is the Valley of Death (Figure 8.1).

The Valley of Death typically occurs at a point between the energy and excitement of setting a strategy or goal, and achieving that strategy or goal in the real world. The journey has five phases.

Phase I—The Start: At first, your excitement is high. The vision is appealing, and you can't wait to get started.

Phase II—The Thrill: You share the vision with others. They get excited too! Energy levels continue to rise. If energy dips this early in the project, this is a red flag that you need to find a more inspiring and optimistic team.

Phase III—The Slide: You start the work. Progress is slow, obstacles are big, and energy is gradually draining.

Phase IV—The Slog: Every day requires enormous effort to make a small amount of progress. It feels like wading through a dense

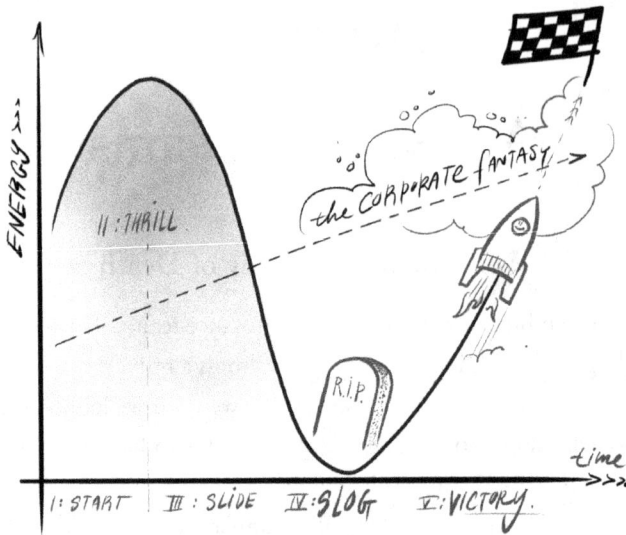

Figure 8.1 The Valley of Death: why strategies fail

swamp while wearing clown shoes. This is where dreams and projects die.

Phase V—The Victory: If you make it through the Slog, success becomes inevitable. You have passed through the Valley of Death, and energy skyrockets. You're exuberant—you made it.

This journey is called the Valley of Death because countless goals, strategies, and dreams have died in the Slog. It's the graveyard of ambition. The Valley of Death adheres to two ironclad rules:

1. The more ambitious and significant the goals, the longer and deeper the Valley of Death.
2. The Valley of Death is inevitable. It's the price you must pay to achieve success.

Unfortunately, most organizations don't prepare for the Valley of Death. When I help them with strategy execution, my first question is: "What's the strategy for your strategy?" In other words, how do you plan to cross the Valley of Death? Usually, I get a wide-eyed look, and after a brief and uncomfortable silence the executives explain that their approach is to move in a straight line from The Start to The Victory. I call this approach the Corporate Fantasy.

As leaders, our goal is to prepare our organizations for the inevitable setbacks they'll encounter while crossing the Valley of Death. This is the core of creating high-performance teams. Busy leaders who choose to go it alone become even busier because they must not only do everything themselves but also because they have no one to turn to when stuck in the Valley of Death. However, simply having a team does not guarantee success. The leader's duty is not only to assemble a team but to activate and motivate the team as well. This means raising team energy, especially when they hit the Slog in the Valley of Death.

When this activation step is missing, you don't have a team, but merely a committee. A committee may share the same goals, but rarely do they share resources or wins and losses collectively. A case in point is the year-end bonuses distributed by many companies. If some employees receive bonuses while others don't, it's not a team.

A real example of a team is the flight crew of a plane crossing the Pacific. They share a common goal (to arrive safely), share resources (the co-pilot steps in during emergencies, even if she is on a break), and win or lose together (an obvious point). The remarkable thing is that these teams operate as one unit, even though the individual team members may change with each flight. The reason is that they embrace a common set of behaviors. They operate in a success environment. A success environment is created when every team member has the opportunity to contribute their best. It invites and nurtures high performance. The key to creating a success environment is to eliminate everything that is not conducive to success.

Let's take a look at the most important parts of a success environment for high-performance teams and what needs to be eliminated if it isn't helpful.

Shared and Ambitious Goals

Here's an exercise I often do with teams. At the start of a team meeting, I ask members to take out a blank sheet of paper and write down, in 30

seconds, the most important goals of the team for the year. Then I col-
lect all the notes and share them with the group. There are two possible
outcomes. The first, and rarest, is that every single team member writes
down the same goals, in the same order, using the same language. More
often than not, I find multiple goals, with varying priorities, and different terminologies. It's not uncommon for a team of five people to list 15
different goals.

This exercise reveals a few things.

When you're challenged to come up with goals in 30 seconds, you use
your subconscious mind, which operates 24/7 and never sleeps. What's
in the subconscious determines focus and usually gets done. If you have
a week to complete the challenge, you access the conscious part of your
brain, which analyzes logically. You also have time to talk with others
about what the goals should be. The 30-second exercise, with its limita-
tions, is therefore an effective way to determine your own focus and that
of your team members.

Second, it immediately shows if the team is aligned in its goals. If it's
not, you don't have a team.

Third, it clarifies priorities. When tough decisions and sacrifices are
required, the lowest-priority goal will be the first to go. If people have
different lowest-priority goals, they will sacrifice different things.

Fourth, a lack of common language indicates a lack of clarity about
the goal itself. For example, "growth in Asia-Pacific" differs from "growth
in China, Japan, and Australia."

Fifth, it reveals how big the team is thinking. A list of incremental
goals indicates a different ambition level than a list of innovative and challenging goals. Ambition is important because it propels people through
difficult times.

Finally, it provides a bridge to connect organizational goals with
personal ones. People act for their own reasons, not someone else's.
Ideally, organizational and personal goals are perfectly aligned. Leaders
need to ask the following question: "If we achieve these goals as a team,
how will this help you achieve your personal goals?" The more detailed
and enthusiastic the answer, the easier it is to keep team members mo-
tivated. The role of a leader is to eliminate any confusion about the
team goals.

Skin in the Game

If the leader is not fully committed, the team will not be either. When you have bacon and eggs for breakfast, the chicken is involved, but the pig is committed.

In 1802, E. I. du Pont founded a gunpowder company, which later became the Fortune 500 company DowDuPont. Manufacturing gunpowder is risky business, but Du Pont built his house within the blast radius of the factory. This ensured that he and his family faced the same risks as the workers. That's called having skin in the game. It means that no one should be involved in any decision if they are shielded from its negative consequences. For example, a company CEO risks bankruptcy if a key business decision goes wrong. Therefore, key business decisions should be hers to make. Similarly, a ship captain will go down with the ship in a catastrophe, so the captain makes the final decision to leave port.

When leaders don't have skin in the game, organizations quickly devolve into hotbeds of recklessness, greed, and unintelligent decision making. The 2008 financial crisis is a case in point. Before the crisis, reckless financial institutions made hefty profits, yet when the financial system collapsed, they had no skin in the game. They kept their profits, while taxpayers bore the cost through system-wide bailouts. In an organization with full commitment, every team member has skin in the game. They speak with One Voice and no one gets a pass.

Helping Each Other Improve

How do you help smart and successful people become even better? Improving the performance of others is a delicate operation. The issue is often that we have great ideas for how to do it but we encounter resistance. Why? Before I answer that question we need to understand that ideas for improvement can either be solicited (based on an explicit request) or unsolicited (spontaneous observations). Ideas for improvement are also based on either the past (observed behavior) or the future (general ideas for improvement).With these two dimensions in mind, we can create a simple framework (Figure 8.2):

Back to our question about meeting resistance. This framework tells a clear story. Unsolicited advice is often perceived as criticism or

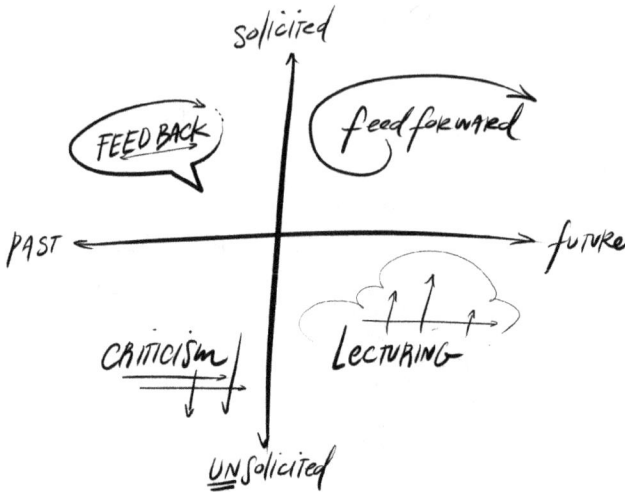

Figure 8.2 How to help others improve

lecturing, which is ineffective. As a leader, ensure that your ideas come in response to an explicit request. When it's about observed behavior, this is feedback. The greatest opportunity for improvement lies in engaging in feedforward—focusing on how things can be done better in the future. The next time you want improvement in an area, such as time management, ask a few trusted friends or colleagues for their best ideas. Then, pick one or two and start implementing them. A team culture of solicited feedback and the use of the feedforward approach reduces resistance, builds trust, and increases performance. As a leader, set the expectation that every team member is committed to helping others improve.

Celebrate Success

Negative self-talk is a psychological phenomenon where a person consistently criticizes or devalues themselves. It focuses on weaknesses in an unhelpful way. What's true for individuals is also true for teams. An organization focused on compensating for weaknesses, rather than building on strengths, will achieve neither. Negative self-talk includes patterns like catastrophizing, thinking in extremes, and making broad negative conclusions based on a single event. It's generally agreed that a healthy ratio of positive to negative feedback is about 3:1. As a leader, this means that the amount of positive praise and support should significantly outweigh negative feedback.

Typical characteristics of a culture not focused on strengths include:

- Performance management focuses on weaknesses instead of on developing strengths.
- Individual success is measured across a broad range of skills instead of key strengths.
- All individuals are assessed based on the same set of skills.

Celebrating success for a leader involves actively looking for opportunities to genuinely acknowledge both individual and team contributions.

Anticipate Mistakes and Blunders

An essential part of creating a successful environment is allowing and expecting team members to make small mistakes while striving for big, ambitious goals. If you punish people for small mistakes, you create a culture of fear and paralysis.

To be effective, we first need to understand the difference between a mistake and a blunder. Some time ago, I decided to drill a hole in my wall to hang a picture. The walls of our house are over a 100 years old, consisting of a mix of plaster, bricks, and small pebbles. At one point, my drill hit a hard stone, got stuck, and my neat little hole was completely ruined. I had made a mistake. Instead of acknowledging that I didn't have the right tools for the job, I convinced myself that I had just been unlucky. So, I decided to drill a new hole using the same ineffective tools. I repeated this approach several times, slowly transforming a once-pristine wall into a bizarre mosaic resembling a heap of rubble. No picture was big enough to cover the disaster I had created. This is the very definition of a blunder. Lesson learned: When you try to correct a small mistake by doubling down, the inevitable result is an epic blunder.

This is common in business, too; we double down on failed products, wrong hires, or disastrous acquisitions. This behavior is based on the sunk cost fallacy: A decision to proceed with a project is not based on the chance of success but on the amount of resources already committed. This happens to the best of us. In 2013, Microsoft bought Nokia's phone business. Despite facing declining sales and market share, Microsoft continued investing in Nokia's mobile phone division for a few years. Eventually, Microsoft had to write off nearly the entire value of the acquisition.

Blunders also include serious errors that jeopardize the continuity of the organization. Examples include going bankrupt, causing harm to people, or facing legal consequences. Additionally, a blunder can be a mistake that is repeated, indicating the organization is unable to learn from its errors. If you want to inspire your team to test new ideas, start a frank conversation about the mistakes you expect them to make and the blunders you expect them to avoid. Then give them the freedom to test many ideas, make many mistakes, and create real impact.

Clear Decision Making

You will only get a consistent and predictable outcome with a system or process. Good decision making in a team starts with having a decision-making process. This involves not only the quality of the decision but also the commitment and support of the team to the decision. As a leader, you must balance control over the decision with the team's commitment to it. The impact of this balance in decision making is described in the Figure 8.3.

Starting at the top, we notice the following:

First level: The leader decides. This typically happens with critical decisions, such as firing a management team member.

Second level: The leader consults individual team members, who provide input, after which the leader decides.

Third level: The leader consults the entire team, then makes a final decision.

Fourth level: The decision is made by team consensus. Every team member can live with the outcome, though it may not be ideal for everyone.

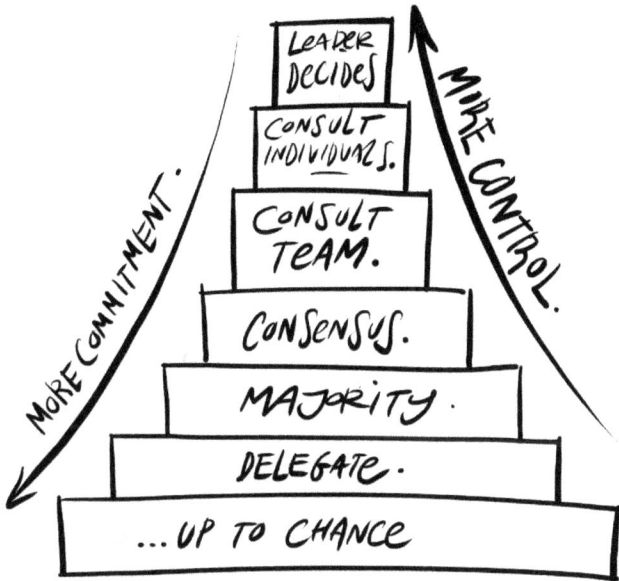

Figure 8.3 The Decision-Making Ziggurat: how to balance control and commitment in decision making

Fifth level: The decision is made by majority vote. If the leader is in the minority, she has given up control over the decision.

Sixth level: The decision is ignored and delegated to circumstances.

Seventh level: The decision is delegated to chance (e.g., a coin flip).

The vast majority of decisions hardly move the needle, so save your energy for more important ones.

Notice that a higher level gives the leader more control over the decision, while a lower level increases the team's commitment.

At what level should decisions be made? In the animated film "Shrek" the villain Lord Farquaad makes a humorous but revealing statement, "Some of you may die on this quest, but that's a risk I'm willing to take." This highlights an important point: A crucial aspect of improving decision making is that decisions should be made by those who face the most significant consequences if the decision is wrong. For instance, if you're considering purchasing a new forklift for your warehouse, it would be wise to let the forklift operators make the final choice within the parameters you've set. The practical application of this approach is to avoid losing control of critical decisions by pushing decision making too low in the organization.

Also, avoid losing team commitment by keeping decision making at the senior management levels.

The most important step in decision making for a leader is to decide at what level a decision should be made and then communicate this transparently to the team.

Ask and Give Help

High-performance leaders don't possess broad strengths in every area relevant to leadership success. For example, Steve Jobs was an innovative visionary. He was also abrasive, rude, and obstinate. To develop impressive strengths in one area, leaders must invest significant time and energy. This means other areas inevitably receive less attention. So, alongside those few impressive strengths, leaders often have many relative weaknesses. To address these weaknesses, leaders typically assemble a team of individuals capable of compensating for their blind spots. But it's not enough to just select talented individuals. As a leader, you also need the vulnerability to ask them for help. "I can do it myself" might work for a 4-year-old, but it has no place in modern business. Most teams are comfortable helping each other. Asking for help, however, is the hardest part. Role-modeling this behavior as a leader is critical.

Drive Innovation

During World War II, a German air raid on the Italian port of Bari accidentally released mustard gas. Medical teams treating the exposed observed an unexpected outcome: significantly reduced white blood cell counts. This unfortunate and surprising effect led pharmacologists to adapt mustard gas into a safer form—nitrogen mustard—and use it to treat lymphoma. The result was groundbreaking: Chemotherapy was born.

Innovation rarely stems from a direct, planned effort. It often arises from tinkering and observing unforeseen events. Mustard gas was developed as a weapon, but its transformation into a lifesaving cancer treatment came from the open-mindedness of researchers who saw potential in an unexpected outcome. The lesson for business leaders is that true innovation requires experimentation and openness to the unexpected. The most groundbreaking ideas often emerge from exploring unplanned results rather than meticulously following a set path.

If you want to build a culture of innovation, encourage your teams to:

- Tinker and test more.
- View surprises not as setbacks but as opportunities.
- Always be curious, not convinced.

Every innovation journey begins with the phrase, "Hmm, that's odd."

Use Supertalents

How do you recognize supertalents? A supertalent is a skill in which you have achieved complete mastery. Examples include project management, problem-solving, or language learning. The challenge is that we are often so proficient with our supertalents that using them comes naturally. As a result, we often underestimate or fail to recognize the power of our own supertalent. We assume that if it's easy for us, everyone else can do it too. If you want to identify your personal supertalent, or the supertalents of your team members, look for three signs:

- You rely on your supertalent whenever you face a complex problem or an exciting opportunity.
- People frequently come to you for help in the area of your supertalent.
- You love to immerse yourself in new perspectives related to your supertalent. The books you read and the websites you visit likely revolve around it.

Once you understand your supertalent, and those of your team members, set a strategy to use and develop them further. This approach allows you to build on your strengths. After all, it's much easier to double down on your strengths than to incrementally improve your weaknesses.

Key Actionable Takeaways

1. **Eliminate the Corporate Fantasy**: Stop expecting progress to follow a straight path from vision to success. Prepare teams for setbacks by removing unrealistic expectations and addressing the inevitable challenges in the Valley of Death.

2. **Remove Passive Involvement**: Avoid confusing involvement with commitment. Dismiss team members who fail to fully engage or lack accountability to ensure everyone has "skin in the game."

3. **End Excessive Goal Setting**: Stop overloading teams with scattered objectives. Focus on a few ambitious, clearly aligned goals that inspire high performance and collaboration.

4. **Abolish Committees Without Accountability**: Disband committees that fail to share resources or responsibilities. Replace them with activated teams that share wins, losses, and a unified purpose.

5. **Do Away with Insulated Decision Makers**: Remove decision makers who are shielded from the consequences of their choices. Ensure that those making high-stakes decisions are directly impacted by the outcomes.

6. **Cut Unsolicited Feedback**: Stop giving feedback that hasn't been requested. Use future-focused feedforward techniques to promote growth and reduce resistance.

7. **Stop Punishing Small Mistakes**: Avoid creating a culture of fear by penalizing minor errors. Allow mistakes to foster learning and experimentation, building a culture of innovation.

8. **Simplify Overly Complex Decision Making**: Remove unnecessary decision layers. Delegate decisions to the lowest competent authority, empowering faster and more effective action.

9. **Eliminate Fixed Innovation Plans**: Ditch rigid frameworks that restrict creative processes. Encourage tinkering, experimentation, and the exploration of unexpected opportunities.

10. **End Negative Self-talk in Teams**: Replace a focus on weaknesses with a strengths-based approach. Shift performance discussions to celebrate wins and cultivate a positive, high-energy environment.

CHAPTER 9

Radical Resilience

Barking Up the Wrong Tree

In his books "Good to Great" and "Built to Last," Jim Collins identified dozens of companies considered high-performing. Almost 30 years later, many of these companies performed much worse than average. Examples include Sony, Ford, and Motorola. Current high performance is no guarantee of future high performance.

So what is? The probability of future greatness is maximized by performing well on the metrics that make an organization less fragile and more resilient: the ability to withstand large shocks to the system. An example of a strong indicator of a robust organization is its internal safety performance, which indicates how many employees are hurt on the job. The reason is that safety performance is an intrinsic organizational value, though it is rarely used for marketing to the outside world. When was the last time you bought an appliance from a company based on its outstanding internal safety record? Other intrinsic values, such as diversity, sustainability, or quality, are typically used for external marketing and communication. This makes them vulnerable to misinterpretation, exaggeration, or even fraud. Thus, we face the problem that many organizational measures are useless to assess and improve resilience. We're barking up the wrong tree. A different approach is needed.

You're More Vulnerable Than You Think

To understand the vulnerabilities of an organization, let's look at the Figure 9.1.

Figure 9.1 describes the impact of events on an organization. It plots cause, known versus unknown; and effect, negative versus positive.

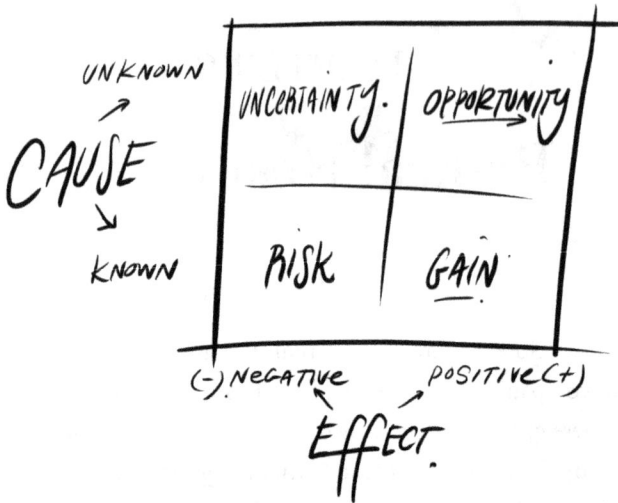

Figure 9.1 The Outcome Oracle: how to improve organizational resilience

Let's take a look at the four quadrants:

1. Uncertainty: If the cause is unknown and its effect is negative, we are dealing with uncertainty. Deterioration of the business environment in the United States can have many causes, but its effect will be negative on your U.S. strategic expansion plans regardless.
2. Opportunity: If the cause is unknown and its effect is positive, we are dealing with opportunity—an influencer who, for mysterious reasons, picks up your product and helps it go viral.
3. Risk: If the cause is known and its effect is negative, we are dealing with risk. A successful challenge from a competitor to your patent could lead to hefty compensation fines.
4. Gain: If the cause is known and its effect is positive, we are dealing with gain. A successful new product will add significantly to the bottom line.

This matrix tells us that if we want to create a more resilient organization, we want to operate more on the right side of the matrix and less on the left side. Resilience hinges on more exposure to positive effects and less exposure to negative effects, regardless of the cause.

This means that we can use three approaches to make our organization more resilient:

1. Create additional options to increase exposure to positive effects. For example, a large innovation portfolio gives us more chances to hit the jackpot.
2. Reduce the factors that reduce optionality and make the organization less resilient—a strategy that depends on the success of a single new product is destined to fail.
3. Reduce the factors that amplify the negative effects of events. An organization with a heavy debt burden (= weakness) may spiral out of control in an economic downturn (= negative event).

To improve resilience, focus on identifying and removing structural weaknesses that either close the door on options or amplify organizational vulnerabilities. Let's take a closer look at the root cause of organizational weaknesses.

Enter the Echo Chamber

As we grow older, the biggest health risk for our teeth is no longer erosion, decay, or cavities. Instead, it's gum health. When gums deteriorate, recede, or become infected, our teeth lose their anchoring and stability. The same is true for mature organizations and mature leaders: As we gain more experience, the issues that limit our performance are no longer missing skills or making unnecessary mistakes. What often holds us back is the lack of a support system within a structured success environment that enables us to do our best work. A success environment provides the experienced executive and seasoned professional with fresh thinking, honest feedback, and positive encouragement. This is not always easy; senior leaders are often the loneliest people in any organization. They need to role-model an uplifting spirit, yet where do they turn when they want to share their doubts and insecurities? They run the risk of operating in an echo chamber.

Insulated leadership accelerates three behaviors that decrease optionality, amplify weaknesses, and hollow out resilience:

1. Arrogance: the belief that there is nothing more to learn. Some years ago, Goldman Sachs landed in hot water when it became clear that several senior executives were using the derogatory term "Muppets" to describe unsophisticated clients internally. The effect on its culture was toxic and destructive.

2. Ignorance: the belief that what you see is all there is. BlackBerry dominated the early smartphone market but ignored data about user preferences for touchscreens and app ecosystems, which the iPhone capitalized on. BlackBerry's reliance on their keyboard devices and reluctance to adopt modern trends led to its rapid decline.

3. Incompetence: the belief that current success is based on skill, not on luck. The sweet illusion of control overrides the harsh reality of uncertainty. Yahoo once dominated the Internet landscape but was overconfident in its acquisition strategy. They acquired a number of start-ups without a coherent strategy for integration, believing they could control these businesses and leverage them for growth. This illusion of control led to poor integration, wasted resources, and a lack of competitive focus, which allowed Google to dominate search and advertising.

Typical signs of insulated leadership are:

- Leaders are afraid to surround themselves with people who are smarter than they are. Looking smart trumps getting results.
- Leaders avoid challenging their own assumptions and knowledge. Being right is more important than being effective.
- Strategies are based on the assumption that the competition is stagnant or will make foolish decisions.
- External partnerships are executed to overpower and take control.
- Managing risk is outsourced to risk managers.
- Leadership spends more time on internal politics rather than focusing on external challenges.

- Attracting celebrity external talent is seen as more valuable than developing internal talent.

Now let's examine some typical issues that lead to insulated leadership.

The Two Buckets Problem

Imagine you have a bucket full of mud. If you add a teaspoon of soup, it will still be a bucket of mud. Now, reverse the situation. If you add a teaspoon of mud to a bucket of soup, the result is also a muddy bucket. Combining something good with something bad often leads to more bad than good. This principle is particularly relevant in mergers, joint ventures, and team combinations. These combinations are often sold as "bringing the best of both worlds together." That was the hype surrounding the 1998 merger of Daimler and Chrysler. But rather than improving Chrysler's reputation to match Daimler's, or using Daimler's market reach to grow Chrysler, the opposite happened: Chrysler's lower quality affected Daimler's market reach. The merger was doomed from the start.

The reason behind this Two Buckets Problem is mathematical: 1 + 1 has only one correct answer but infinite wrong answers. Bad habits, values, and systems always outnumber and overwhelm the good ones. External orientation and partnerships are not enough to create resilience. You must be very cautious with the people, teams, and organizations you associate with. If you value your soup, stay far away from the mud.

The Deep Dogmas

Not long ago, historians believed civilization in South America developed relatively recently. But the discovery of Chankillo in Peru, the oldest known astronomical observatory in the Americas, proved otherwise. By combining astronomy with carbon dating, researchers found the site to be over 2,300 years old. This is a great example of how mixing different kinds of knowledge can lead to major discoveries. A similar phenomenon happened when magnetic resonance imaging (MRI), derived from physics, revolutionized medical science. These advances occur when outside experts challenge Deep Dogmas—the long-held internal assumptions within every professional field.

So consider:

- How well do you challenge the Deep Dogmas in your own industry? Are your diversity efforts truly effective, or are they replacing one set of Deep Dogmas with another?
- How much time does your organization spend on external orientation? Different disciplines from the outside world challenge our ways of thinking.

The death of a Deep Dogma is a tremendous opportunity for advancement.

Confronting Taboo Topics

Real vulnerability in an organization often stems from a Taboo Topic: a significant issue that cannot be discussed openly, such as:

- A failing merger that, despite increasing resources, will never succeed.
- A strategic direction that depends on a miraculous market turnaround.
- A charismatic CEO whose toxic behavior is eroding trust within the company.
- Costly new assets that are flawed by design.
- The hope that a formidable competitor will make irrational decisions.
- An IT system that promised speed but delivers frustration and inefficiency.
- Utopian company targets that demotivate rather than inspire.
- A new hire whose incompetence is becoming increasingly obvious.

Reality is not what we want it to be, wish it to be, or expect it to be. Reality simply is—and must be acknowledged honestly and courageously.

What is the one significant issue in your organization that remains a Taboo Topic?

Petrified Performance Standards

Some time ago, traffic engineers found that pedestrian accident rates involving children were higher at certain intersections. They discovered that drivers subconsciously used the height of the person crossing the road to judge distance. Since children are shorter, they appeared further away than they were, giving drivers less reaction time. The solution was to place physical objects like waste bins and streetlights near the crossing to help drivers better gauge distance.

Similarly, if you lack external reference points for your performance or that of your organization, you may fall into the trap of petrified performance standards—standards inferior to those of your peers, clients, or competitors.

Typical signs include:

- Difficulty finding new employment for people from your organization.
- Difficulty retaining top talent.
- A leadership team that only promotes from within.
- Underperformance that is tolerated.
- Clients that leave quickly when the opportunity arises.
- Suspicious attitudes toward outside help.

One of the most effective ways to improve executive and organizational performance is to create a system that provides a systematic approach to getting external input from diverse peers to challenge petrified performance standards. Where do you need to place waste bins and streetlights to raise your own performance standards?

Ignoring Quiet Competence

Plane trips should be uneventful. Excitement and adrenaline are best experienced elsewhere. But for one plane to get from point A to B smoothly, the quietly competent workers in the background must do their jobs well. These individuals, including aircraft fuelers, mechanics, and flight dispatchers, are not flashy, won't be admired on social media, and won't appear on magazine covers. They are very good at what they do, working in the background, showing up every day to give their best. They demonstrate quiet competence. Yet leadership focus and admiration often go to the loudest voices. Quiet competence is the glue that holds every high-performance organization together. Ignoring the quietly competent people is a recipe for disaster.

Overlooking Extraordinary Talent

Let's do a thought experiment. Think of all the executive leaders in your company, those you know and have worked with. Are there any leaders in this group of whom you haven't the foggiest idea how they got there? If there are, how would you explain this?

Let me introduce the Blunt Executive Review Tool (BERT) (Figure 9.2).

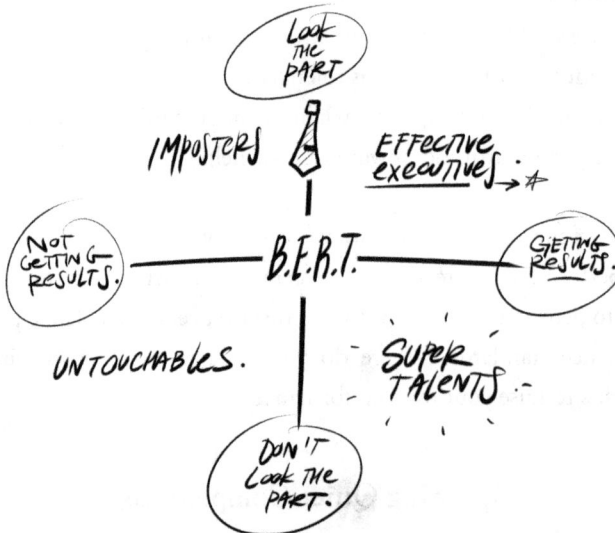

Figure 9.2 The Blunt Executive Review Tool: how to spot Supertalents

This tool reviews leaders on two dimensions:

The first dimension is getting results: How much they contribute to the strategic goals of the company.

The second dimension is looking the part: the appearance, mannerisms, habits, language, and behaviors you expect from your leaders. Naturally, looking the part varies for different types of organizations. T-shirts are natural in start-ups, whereas designer suits are more common in investment banking.

The four categories in our BERT are:

1. The Untouchables: These leaders don't achieve results and don't look the part. They work in the organization because of family ties, legal requirements, or they possess compromising information on important people. I call them untouchables because they are immune to being fired.
2. The Imposters: These leaders look the part but don't get results. They tend to stay in their jobs briefly, always rotating to other organizations just before they're found out.
3. The Effective Executives: These leaders get results and look the part. They are the backbone of any company, reliable, predictable, and consistent.
4. The Supertalents: These leaders get results but don't look the part. They are ... different.

In turbulent times, the focus of any organization should be to spot and nurture its Supertalents. Here's why: Imagine the future of your company depends on marketing a new product. You can choose between two reputable marketing executives with a track record of great achievement. One looks like a successful marketer (great hair, tailored clothes, polished speech), the other doesn't (unkempt hair, ill-fitting clothes, mumbles). Which one would you choose? I would pick the marketing executive who doesn't look the part. They are successful despite negative appearances. This means they must be very good. These people are your real Supertalents.

Developing Supertalents

In the television series "The Mandalorian," Grogu—the small and cute Baby Yoda character—became the pilot of a Gundam—a manned robot that enhanced his powers and enabled him to move and operate much faster and better. This is a proper analogy for an enterprise as well. A Gundam organization is a large organization that creates significant value by enhancing the talents of a few extraordinary individuals. It's based on the idea that a very small group creates almost all future value. For example, a few years ago, a senior Microsoft executive mentioned that less than 1 percent of their software developers are more than 1,000 times more productive than the average software developer. This means that as leaders in a big organization, our focus should not only be to identify but develop those Supertalents. This requires the construction of a Gundam: All systems and processes must be aimed at removing every single hurdle that prevents these star individuals from using their unique talents to create. The DNA of a high-performance enterprise must include developing Supertalents.

The Lag Between Actions and Results

"If you want a quick path to a successful career, become an oil reservoir engineer." This was the first piece of half-joking advice given to me by a grinning reservoir engineer on my first day working for a big oil company. "You can make grand promises about large oil deposits in the ground," he said. "And since actual oil production may take decades, you can create the illusion of vast possibilities and never be held accountable for any errors in your predictions."

There are professions where the time between action and outcome is very short. Absence of skill results in a quick exit from those professions. Very few successful dentists have an extensive track record of bad dentistry. Incompetent plumbers don't get hired. Erratic patisserie chefs end up washing dishes. A key characteristic of skill is repeatable performance.

What about senior executives in large companies? In complex and established organizations, systems and processes run the machine. Individual decisions by senior executives may not matter much in the short term. Climbing the corporate hierarchy leads to more and more time distance between action and result. Significant successes also occur at a very low frequency. How many times can a chief strategy officer engage in multiyear assignments to build a track record of successfully changing the strategic direction of an organization?

This is the Illusion of Competence: The pool of senior executives who have achieved their position based on luck, rather than skill, may be much larger than you think. Developing real skill is all about maintaining a short distance between action and results. Keep this in mind when selecting, developing, and promoting the next generation of leaders. This is your true legacy.

Premortems

Strategy failure often occurs not because of missing knowledge, but because of what we think we know that simply isn't true. These flawed thoughts are assumptions, and they frequently cause great projects to crash and burn. Conducting a premortem on your project helps you avoid falling into this trap. A premortem is the opposite of a postmortem. In a postmortem, mistakes are identified after a project has failed. In a premortem you creatively identify the likely major causes of failure before the project begins by imagining that the project has already failed. This exercise allows you to anticipate roadblocks in advance (thus cheating sudden project death) and significantly increases the success probability of your endeavor.

Here's how a premortem team exercise works:

- Imagine 5 years into the future. Your project has failed so miserably that the Harvard Business Review has asked to interview you about the reasons behind your failure.
- Divide the project team into small subgroups and have each group discuss what would be said in this interview.
- Gather the insights from all subgroups. The combined feedback will provide a clear picture of the main internal project risks.
- Mitigate risks by incorporating these insights into the project design from the very start.

Key Actionable Takeaways

1. **Dismantle Deep Dogmas**: Eliminate entrenched beliefs that hinder innovation. Challenge assumptions with fresh, external perspectives to foster breakthroughs and improved resilience.

2. **Avoid Toxic Partnerships**: Do not engage in alliances or mergers that combine inferior elements with strong ones, risking the dilution of quality and success. Select partnerships that elevate, not contaminate.

3. **Disrupt Leadership Echo Chambers**: Remove the isolation that arises from insulated leadership. Foster environments that encourage honest feedback and diverse viewpoints to enhance decision making.

4. **Expose False Competence**: Challenge the assumption that seniority equates to skill. Remove barriers to revealing true abilities by linking actions with measurable outcomes.

5. **Eliminate Focus on Superficial Traits**: Avoid prioritizing appearance or conventional expectations in talent selection. Focus on identifying and nurturing extraordinary individuals who achieve remarkable results.

6. **End Tolerance for Taboo Topics**: Stop ignoring significant issues that undermine resilience, such as flawed strategies or toxic leadership. Address these problems directly to strengthen organizational foundations.

7. **Remove Overreliance on Internal Standards**: Avoid petrified performance standards by introducing external benchmarks. This ensures your team measures success against evolving market and industry expectations.

8. **Elevate Quiet Competence**: Stop overlooking individuals who perform essential tasks consistently in the background. Recognize and reward their contributions to build a stronger organizational core.

9. **Break the Illusion of Control**: Eliminate strategies that assume predictable competition or luck-based outcomes. Build adaptive systems to navigate uncertainty and foster sustainable growth.

10. **Simplify and Premortem**: Remove the guesswork by conducting premortems to anticipate potential failures. This proactive approach minimizes risks and ensures more resilient strategies.

CHAPTER 10

Your Legacy

A Trail or a Legacy?

Hewlett-Packard was once a model of innovation and a symbol of Silicon Valley success. The company embraced a culture known as "The HP Way," which emphasized decentralized management, employee autonomy, innovation, and a commitment to quality. However, over the years, HP drifted from these founding principles. In 2015, Hewlett-Packard split into two companies. The current combined revenue of the two Hewlett-Packard entities is less than 70 percent of its former peak. This is an example of an organization that was unable to maintain its original DNA. Its leaders of the past 20 years left a trail but didn't leave a legacy. A legacy is determined by what is left when you, as a leader, are gone. Interestingly, a focus on your legacy can be a catalyst to accomplish more by doing less. It starts with building systems. You will only get predictable and consistent results with a process or a system.

This explains why lottery winners and heirs of significant fortunes often live in a state of permanent anxiety: They know that their success is not repeatable. If they lose their wealth, they don't have a system in place to get it back.

To maximize the immediate benefit of all our systems, we need to ask ourselves the following questions:

- What's the most important issue in your organization? Who is currently building a system to deal with this issue?
- Where are your results still shaky and haphazard? What do you need to change in your process to improve?
- If you could change one process in your organization to accelerate your results, which would it be?

The objective of any strategic project is to build a process or system. How would you define the scope of your strategic projects with this outcome in mind? Since the success of any strategy is defined by simply not failing, the best strategy execution plans are based on building a system that avoids failure. How well have you incorporated this approach into your current strategy execution plan? For example, if you don't have a process for selling, you're at the mercy of someone else's process for buying. Where does your sales success depend on the process of others?

Systems and processes are the superpowers of any high-performance individual, team, or organization. How can you use these superpowers to focus on the longer term and cement your legacy?

The Legacy Pyramid

Let's look at the Figure 10.1.

It describes the hierarchy of responsibility of the leaders in your organization. Starting at the top we see the following:

Level 1: Legacy Responsibility. Leadership is defined as making yourself obsolete.

Level 2: Behavioral Responsibility. Leaders define shared standards and extensively role-model them throughout the organization, regularly crossing functions and silos.

Level 3: Strategic Responsibility. In this case, the focus is on achieving the overall strategy of the organization. Typically, functional goals are sacrificed to achieve the overall goals of the organization.

Level 4: Functional Responsibility. The main objective is to ensure that a function in the organization, such as HR, finance, or IT, runs smoothly. Success is determined by achieving the goals of the function itself.

There is a fascinating application of this pyramid: You can't solve a structural issue at the level where the effect of the issue consistently occurs. Whenever I help a leadership team improve strategy execution, my first request is for them to rate their strategy execution power versus their

LeADeRSHIP·
ReSPONSIBILITIES:

SeTTING
BeHAVIORAL STANDARDS.

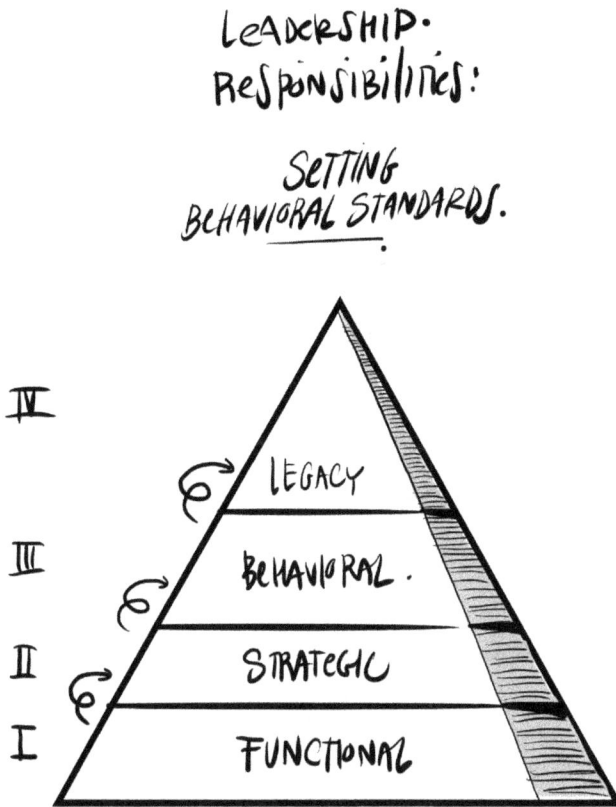

Figure 10.1 The Legacy Pyramid: how to elevate leadership focus

functional execution power. In other words, is the execution issue broad across the organization, or is it limited to the strategy alone? Even in successful organizations, functional execution is often up to standard, but strategy execution is much more difficult. If this is the case, you can't solve it at the strategy execution level. Better strategy execution systems or strategy communication plans will not solve these structural issues. What's lacking are the behavioral standards senior leaders need to align with organizational strategy—such as sharing resources or sacrificing functional goals to achieve organizational goals.

This also implies that shifting your focus to taking responsibility for building a legacy not only creates a more robust future for the organization but improves immediate overall performance as well. What are the most important issues to consider when you want to build a legacy?

Behavior Versus Process

Here is an interesting question: At which level does your team solve problems?

The first level is content focus. Content focus means changing a thing:

- If the motor is broken, change the motor.
- If the team is underperforming, expand the team.
- If customer satisfaction is too low, use new technology to improve quality control.

When structural problems keep occurring, we move to the second level, which is process focus. It means changing a system to change a thing:

- If the motor keeps breaking, change the selection process for a new motor to include different quality criteria.
- If the team is underperforming again, change the search process to hire a more effective new team member.
- If customer satisfaction is down again, change the scouting system for new and innovative technologies to improve quality control.

When teams become very good at solving problems by process, this typically becomes their default approach to fixing issues. Yet we can't solve a structural issue at the level where it appears. Thus, we don't solve a structural process issue by simply adding more processes.

What we need is a third level to solve problems. This level involves setting new behavioral standards.

Which new behavioral standards do we need to set to:

- Avoid the motor breaking again? Take ownership to do preventive maintenance.
- Avoid the team underperforming again? Get rid of kryptonite behaviors that drain team energy.
- Avoid customer satisfaction being down again? Fall in love with your customers, to serve them better, and go the extra mile.

The third level of problem-solving is rare, yet it is one of the most powerful ways to create a legacy that will consistently take your team's performance to the next level. Unfortunately, there are a few unhelpful mindsets and behaviors that will put a wrench in your best-laid legacy plans.

Negative Nudging

Imagine a world where the number of hospitals is intentionally reduced. Would this scarcity nudge people toward a healthier lifestyle? My hunch says, probably not. Moreover, the collateral damage of such a decision would become quickly apparent: Fewer hospitals will result in more sick people. This brings us to a curious exploration of negative nudging—a tactic where leaders attempt to steer behavior by penalizing undesired actions. But does this approach drive our habits in the intended direction?

A newly developed suburb in the Netherlands was intentionally designed with a scarcity of parking spots. The thinking was that residents would adapt and use their cars less. Instead, it caused a perpetual state of chaos, with neighbors fighting each other for each precious parking spot. Negative nudging seems to fail when the unintended consequences of the cure are worse than the illness. If your legacy goal is to amplify positive behavior, eliminate the barriers that inhibit people from taking the desired actions. Take sales, for instance. If you aim to grow sales, obliterate every obstacle for your clients to buy, such as exhaustive digital payment steps, nonsupportive customer service, and pushy salespeople.

Worshipping at the Altar of Best Practices

Is the love for best practices key to long-term success? The Von Foerster Theorem, a cornerstone of the intriguing field of cybernetics, illustrates how systems can evolve from randomness or chaos into complexity and order, often through positive feedback loops.

Consider rush-hour traffic. It self-organizes, transitioning from disorder (individual, uncoordinated vehicle movements) to a higher order (coordinated flow, formation of lanes), driven by the interactions among its components (vehicles and drivers). This theorem suggests that more restrictions reduce the impact of individual parts on the system. For instance, if cars were linked like train wagons, adapting to changing circumstances would be much more challenging. This concept applies to best practices as well. The more rigid and extensive the practices, the less responsive an organization becomes to changing environments. Bearing this in mind, a potent strategy for business growth is to acquire companies and take full control of their financial steering but leave them entirely independent in all other aspects. Making an organization more resilient doesn't necessarily mean adopting more best practices. On the contrary, it often involves eliminating any current best practice that may optimize the system but are not critical for future success. An organization that is afraid of killing off best practices will find itself inflexible and stuck in the long run.

Leave Excellence Alone

In 1985, Coca-Cola introduced a supposedly improved version of its wildly successful soft drink, called New Coke. It was a complete disaster. After howls of protest and collapsing sales, the company hastily backtracked and returned to its original Coke recipe. This historical blunder is like trying to enhance the Mona Lisa with finger-paint. This type of behavior is driven by a deadly combination of arrogance, incompetence, and ignorance. A helpful approach to avoid tampering with what works well is to understand the Lindy effect: The future life expectancy, value, and usefulness of an item, technology, or idea is proportional to its current age. For example, the works of Shakespeare have been in print for hundreds of years, and it's very likely that they will still be in print hundreds of years from now. If an item, technology, or idea has a track record of large value, proven usefulness, and long staying power, it's probably best to leave it alone and focus your efforts on something else. Instead of trying to improve an existing masterpiece, focus on creating a new masterpiece of your own.

Strive for Broad Excellence

There are three important rules if you want to grow as a leader.

The first rule is that it's much easier to build on strengths than to compensate for weaknesses. This is only natural, as we need far less energy to become twice as powerful in areas of strength versus trying to become 10 percent stronger in areas of weakness. The idea that you grow by compensating for your weaknesses is folly. As we noted earlier, if you spend a lifetime compensating for your weaknesses, you end up with a large set of strong weaknesses.

The second rule is that the more profound your abilities, the more profound your weaknesses. The reason is simple: It takes a lot of time and energy to develop extraordinary skills. Popular thinking suggests it takes 10,000 hours to become a master. Though this number is often disputed, the point remains the same. The time spent building strengths was not spent learning other things.

The third rule is that profound abilities and strengths will rise to the surface when behaviors that hide strengths are eliminated. It's not uncommon to read stories about individuals in poor physical condition who decide to get serious about health and end up running marathons. At the same time, they also start to exhibit great success in their chosen professions or careers. The behaviors that hid their strengths were eliminated, allowing their strengths to surface.

Successful leaders, therefore, don't try to gain broad excellence. They achieve extraordinary success by making a conscious choice to accentuate their strengths. How can you achieve that?

A distillation column is an industrial piece of equipment designed to separate components. It consists of a series of stacked plates. Separation of the components occurs by selective boiling and condensation on each plate. The distillation process is a fitting approach to grow rapidly and scale your results. It's applicable to leaders as well. If you take stock of everything you do, which activities are you doing so well that they should never be done by anyone else? This is your best work. Delegate, eliminate, or outsource everything else. If you build a system for your leaders that allows them to apply this professional distillation process systematically, more and more of their time will be concentrated on using and expanding their Supertalents.

The difference between good results and extraordinary results boils down to professional distillation: the ability to avoid stagnation by a continuous process of separating good work from your best work.

Succumbing to Imposter Syndrome

A live-action role-playing game (LARP) is an activity where participants physically portray their (fictional) characters. It's weirdly fun. However, LARPing is not limited to the world of entertainment. In the professional world, the technical term for LARPing is imposter syndrome: the dreaded feeling that you're pretending to be an accomplished professional. At any moment, people may find out, expose you, and force you to resign in shame.

Imposter syndrome is widespread and affects even the most accomplished leaders. Its root cause is a self-image that is not aligned with your accomplishments. If your self-image is bigger than your accomplishments, you may act arrogant and smug. If your self-image is smaller than your accomplishments, you may act timid and afraid. This negatively impacts your performance.

There are three keys to getting over imposter syndrome and improving your self-image:

- You can't fail unless you decide to no longer contribute to improving the condition of others. This is the standard you should use to judge yourself.
- Be clear about your goals and focus on taking action. The definition of happiness is continuous progress toward worthy objectives.
- Don't minimize your supertalents: You're so good at your profession that you think your skills are ordinary and everybody is capable of doing what you do. Always recognize and appreciate the unique skillset that took years of hard work to build.

Always remember that you're not an actor pretending to be an executive. You're an executive performing on the big stage.

How Much Is Enough?

In June 2012, Rajat Gupta was convicted on insider trading charges. As a former CEO of McKinsey, he was already a very wealthy man. Yet he engaged in criminal activities to become even wealthier. Why? It was reported that Gupta, as a decamillionaire, often hung out with billionaires. This made him feel that he didn't have enough.

A great danger for successful people is being unclear about how much is enough. When are you done? If you're unclear about this, you will continue throwing additional resources into doing more or getting more. This can make you lose perspective and expose yourself to unnecessary risks.

If you run a business and haven't decided what revenue you want to earn this year, you never stop working: There's always another dollar to be made. If you want to develop a new product and haven't decided what the minimum specs would look like, you will continue to improve without launching. If you decide to create a new strategy but haven't set a deadline, you will never stop doing additional research.

Boundaries, limits, and deadlines on positive developments are essential for high performance: They help you shift perspective from perfection to success.

Going Lame

Going lame is a term used to describe a high-performing racehorse that suddenly can't perform at the top of its game. This can be caused by injury, trauma, or the passing of time. This also happens to high-performing executives. While performing at their peak, they suddenly slow down and are surpassed by others. For executives, this often means receiving a generous package to exit the company.

Going lame is the inevitable fate for all of us. Everything we do has a shelf life—especially when we operate at peak performance. Our focus should therefore be on preparing for our next adventure. We need to be gone before we are done.

Executives who have successfully made this shift in thinking often provide even more value by adopting very different roles. They expand their legacy outside the organization by finding a niche where they can combine their Supertalents with their vast experience. For example, they become part of an advisory board, operate as angel investors, or take on high-level teaching or consulting roles.

You're not bound to your current racetrack, even if you're number 1 and look invincible.

Key Actionable Takeaways

1. **Eliminate Short-Term Focus**: Stop focusing on temporary wins or activity trails. Build systems and processes designed to persist and deliver value long after you are gone.

2. **Remove Excessive Processes**: Avoid solving structural issues by layering on more processes. Focus on setting new behavioral standards that drive meaningful, long-term change.

3. **Discard Outdated Best Practices**: Let go of rigid best practices that hinder adaptability and innovation. Remove those that no longer align with future goals or evolving circumstances.

4. **Stop Negative Nudging**: Avoid penalizing undesired behaviors, as it often leads to unintended consequences. Instead, remove barriers to enable positive actions and foster growth.

5. **Eliminate the Illusion of Competence**: Challenge systems that rely on appearances or luck instead of measurable results. Replace them with processes that tie actions directly to outcomes.

6. **Know When to Stop**: Define clear boundaries and limits for goals and objectives. Shift from endless pursuit to focusing on sustainable, meaningful success.

7. **Avoid Overtampering with Excellence**: Resist the urge to improve well-functioning systems or products unnecessarily. Focus your efforts on creating new areas of impact rather than altering proven successes.

8. **Remove Barriers to Supertalents**: Strip away obstacles that prevent exceptional individuals from maximizing their impact. Build environments that amplify their abilities and results.

9. **Avoid Perfectionism Traps**: Let go of unachievable perfection and focus on timely, effective actions that bring meaningful results. Perfection often delays progress and wastes resources.

10. **Prepare for Transitions Before They Are Forced**: Anticipate the shelf life of your peak performance. Exit roles strategically to continue adding value in new capacities and leave behind a robust legacy.

Epilogue: The Art of Subtraction

Complexity is self-inflicted and most leaders are their own worst enemies. Success doesn't come from more–better–faster; it comes from eliminating what no longer works. This isn't just efficient—it's transformative.

This book has given you the tools to cut through the clutter and focus on what drives results. Now, it's up to you to act.

If you want to achieve the extraordinary, stop rationalizing mediocrity and boldly focus on:

- **Dismantling Deep Dogmas that cement outdated thinking in your industry.** Challenge entrenched beliefs to uncover breakthroughs, like discovering Chankillo in the sands of South America.
- **Stepping out of the echo chamber that insulates leadership.** Replace yes-men with diverse perspectives to avoid oblivion, as BlackBerry's fall from dominance illustrates.
- **Smashing the Two Buckets Problem in partnerships.** Mixing mud with soup doesn't elevate; it contaminates. Select alliances that amplify, not dilute.
- **Exiting the Valley of Death by eliminating unrealistic expectations.** Big goals aren't straight paths; prepare for the inevitable slog with a strategy for your strategy.
- **Abandoning bloated committees that lack accountability.** Activate teams that share wins, losses, and resources, like a flight crew navigating across oceans.
- **Obliterating complexity in decision-making layers.** Simplify choices by delegating power to those closest to the consequences, whether it's a forklift operator or a frontline innovator.

- **Cutting zombie projects that drain resources long after they've been canceled.** Resurrect focus by ensuring dead ideas stay buried.
- **Ceasing to polish what already shines.** Don't paint over the Mona Lisa; preserve proven excellence and redirect energy to creating new masterpieces.
- **Removing safety nets that insulate decision makers from their outcomes.** If leaders lack skin in the game, they lack the accountability to steer wisely.
- **Discarding negative nudging that punishes unwanted behavior.** Like scarce parking in Dutch suburbs, penalties can create chaos instead of solutions.
- **Halting the worship of rigid best practices.** In a world of rush-hour traffic, flexibility beats standardization when adapting to change.
- **Banishing the Illusion of Competence.** Long gaps between actions and outcomes breed faux expertise. Measure skill with results, not appearances.
- **Decluttering your "golden triangle" of strengths, passions, and value creation.** Drop activities outside this zone to achieve exponential impact.
- **Slashing the noise to focus on the signal.** Don't let fleeting trends or crises drown out your priorities—filter for what truly moves the needle.
- **Uprooting the sunk cost fallacy.** Stop doubling down on failing ideas, whether it's drilling a ruined wall or persisting with a flawed acquisition like Nokia.
- **Questioning taboo topics that fester in silence.** Toxic leadership or utopian goals can't be ignored. Tackle the hard truths to strengthen your foundation.
- **Leaving the race before going lame.** Like retiring a champion racehorse, pivot before your peak fades to redefine success in a new arena.
- **Eliminating Kryptonite behaviors that drain team energy.** Empower teams by setting new standards for ownership and collaboration.

- **Cutting the endless pursuit of "more."** Define "enough" to shift from perfectionism to sustainable success, avoiding the fate of Rajat Gupta's ambition.
- **simplifying processes to drive speed.** Halve meeting durations, unblob objectives, and apply Parkinson's Law to compress timelines effectively.
- **Removing barriers to innovation.** Allow room for tinkering, experimentation, and the serendipity of unexpected breakthroughs.
- **Burning dead wood in performance standards.** Use external benchmarks to prevent stagnation and ensure your metrics remain relevant.
- **Silencing negative self-talk within teams.** Celebrate strengths rather than fixating on weaknesses to foster high-performance environments.
- **Avoiding the imposters in leadership.** Seek results over appearances, nurturing Supertalents who defy conventional expectations.
- **Replacing rigidity with optionality.** Build a portfolio of opportunities to buffer against uncertainty and reduce reliance on singular successes.
- **Setting boundaries to control scope creep.** Whether it's goals, projects, or strategies, limits create clarity and drive focus.
- **Delegating good work to concentrate on your best work.** Apply professional distillation to ensure leaders operate in their zone of greatest impact.
- **Eliminating perfection traps in innovation.** The messy middle often hides the magic. Embrace oddities and surprises as pathways to breakthroughs.
- **Shifting from control to collaboration.** Your team is a symphony, not a solo. Reduce micromanagement and let collective talent shine.
- **Cutting the clutter of competing goals.** Focus energy on fewer, more ambitious objectives to magnify results.
- **Clearing the fog around decision making.** Use premortems to anticipate failure and pivot early, avoiding costly missteps.

- **Removing hero leadership from your playbook.** Teams thrive when leaders foster independence rather than solving every problem themselves.
- **Stopping the habit of reactive leadership.** Proactively define your strategic boundaries and refuse to be ruled by external urgencies.
- **Removing the need to look smart.** Focus on getting results over maintaining appearances to cultivate authentic leadership.
- **Defying the tyranny of short-term wins.** Build systems for enduring success rather than temporary flashes of achievement.
- **Stripping away what doesn't serve your legacy.** A great leader isn't measured by their busyness but by the impact that endures.

And finally, focus **on removing the "non-David" to reveal the masterpiece hidden in your work or organization.** Like Michelangelo's approach to sculpture, real success lies in subtraction, not addition.

PART 2

Acting Differently

The Michelangelo Toolkit

1. The Clarity Sequence: how to effectively engage an organization to create strategic clarity
2. High-Performance Goal Setting: how to avoid common goal-setting mistakes
3. Unlocking Group Intelligence: how to execute a great brainstorm
4. The Creativity Supernova: how to bring creativity and energy to a brainstorm session
5. The Option Development System: how to think systematically to create options
6. The One Page Strategy: how to create a strategy blueprint
7. The Executive Maverick: how to break industry norms to drive innovation
8. Energy Shift: How to focus organizational energy to maximize value creation
9. The Innovation Choice: how to focus on the right type of innovation
10. The Ownership Ladder: how to drive ownership
11. The Smart Decision Grid: how to make better and faster decisions
12. The Decision Catalyst: how to make better team decisions when information is scarce
13. Strategic Quitting: how to do more of your highest and best use of time
14. Strategic Sacrifice: how to do more of your future highest and best use of time
15. Zero-Based Thinking: how to help your team focus on the highest and best use of time
16. High-Impact Meetings: how to build a high-performance meeting culture
17. The Execution Machine: how to build a personal execution engine
18. Ready for Anything: how to improve organizational resilience
19. The Genius Code: how to spot Supertalents

20. The Premortem: how to increase the probability of strategy success
21. The Valley of Death: how to activate teams
22. High-Performance Teams: the nine focus areas to help your team overcome the Valley of Death
23. Raising the Bar: how to help others improve
24. The Decision-Making Ziggurat: how to balance leadership control and team commitment in decision making
25. The Legacy Pyramid: how to elevate leadership focus

1 The Clarity Sequence: how to effectively engage an organization to create strategic clarity

1. Understand what the vision of massive success looks like.
2. Define the behavioral standards necessary to achieve the vision.
3. Engage the organization and brainstorm creative solutions.
4. Organize and structure all ideas and resources in a strategic plan.
5. Take significant action.

2 High-Performance Goal Setting: how to avoid common goal-setting mistakes

1. Aspirational Goals instead of Tangible Goals.
   A goal is defined as something an external observer can clearly identify as achieved or not. It's always directional: moving from one specific state to another.
2. "Meh" Goals instead of Inspiring Goals.
   The best goals are challenging, meaning there's a 50/50 chance of achieving them
3. Good Goals instead of Best Goals.
   The best way to define your goals is to define your "anti-goals." An anti-goal is a goal that is good but not the best.
4. Important Goals instead of Prioritized Goals.
   Your goal priorities will determine what gets sacrificed first.
5. Individual Goals instead of Common Goals.
   Individual goals must align with the team's common goals, and clarity on these common goals is essential.
6. Arbitrary Options instead of Specific Goals.
   Many strategies fail because organizations confuse an option with a goal. The rule is: Be unyielding in your goals but flexible in your options.
7. Project Thinking instead of Portfolio Thinking.
   The essence of portfolio thinking is to develop as many options as possible to achieve your goal, starting with the most promising. Project thinking, on the other hand, is about being complete and accurate.
8. Boundaries instead of Goals.
   A boundary is a condition that must be met under all circumstances; otherwise, your strategy fails. To clarify boundaries, ask: "I have the freedom to do whatever it takes to achieve our strategic goals, provided that ...."

3 Unlocking Group Intelligence: how to execute a great brainstorm

To avoid wasting your own precious time and others' limited energy, stick to the following best practices for your next brainstorm:

First, state the subject clearly at the beginning. The most powerful questions to get creative juices flowing is the Platinum Question consisting of three parts:

1. How can we …
2. While at the same time …
3. So that we …

The first part helps frame the discussion and guide the brainstorming process. The second part establishes boundary conditions. Without clear boundaries, there are no useful ideas, only speculation. The third part of the Platinum Question describes the ultimate objective, allowing you to judge the validity of any idea.

Second, give all participants time to think: Let them generate ideas individually and in silence for at least 10 minutes.

Third, focus on quantity over quality: You need a lot of ideas to end up with a few good ones. To facilitate this, make abundant use of the Magic Question For Thinking Big (MQFTB): "What's even better than this?"

Fourth, define criteria for a "good" idea: At a minimum, a good idea must:

- Provide a solution to a significant issue.
- Be feasible.
- Be effective at solving the problem.
- Have more positives than negatives.

Fifth, close the session with a commitment for next steps:

- Provide a summary of the ideas.
- Describe a process to select the best ideas.
- Give clarity about any further expected involvement of participants.

4 The Creativity Supernova: how to bring creativity and energy to a brainstorm session

1. Parking Lot Magic: Park off-topic subjects separately and revisit them later.
2. Cone of Silence: What happens in the room stays in the room. Trust is key. If participants are afraid to speak due to hierarchy, use anonymous brainstorming (e.g., writing ideas on paper anonymously).
3. Musical Chairs: Swap seats at every break for fresh perspectives.
4. Time Boxing: Set fixed time slots for each topic (e.g., 15 minutes per topic).
5. Grim Reaper Rule: Silence means agreement. This ensures everyone takes ownership.
6. Going Supernova: After each idea, challenge the team with "Can we top this?" to encourage thinking bigger.
7. Dragon Slayer: If consensus is reached too quickly on a difficult topic, dig deeper.
8. Idea Marathon: Generate at least 20 individual ideas before sharing with the group.
9. Silent Brainstorms: Quiet thinking for 10 minutes can spark brilliance, especially for introverted participants.
10. Action Finale: Conclude with crystal-clear steps—who does what and when.

5 The Option Development System: how to think systematically to create options

Since the act of thinking requires a lot of energy, your brain develops automatic thinking patterns when faced with a problem. Getting new and original solutions is therefore difficult. The "20 ways thinking technique" helps bypass these mental barriers to keep generating new ideas. Here's how it works:

Define your problem as a Platinum question on a blank sheet of paper.

1. How can we ...
2. While at the same time ...
3. So that we ...

Write down and number all the possible solutions to this problem.

- If the problem is significant, the first 5 to 10 solutions you write down will be obvious, as they are generated spontaneously by the conscious mind.
- Solutions 10 to 15 will be difficult because they require hard thinking and force you to create new associations. Your initial instinct will be to give up and name a previous solution as ideal. Don't give in to this instinct—continue.
- Solutions 15 to 20 are tough but force yourself to keep going. Oftentimes, the breakthrough insights and creative ideas come in the last five solutions.

6 The One Page Strategy: how to create a strategy blueprint

The strategy blueprint is the North Star for driving consistent execution. It answers the following questions:

- What does remarkable strategic success look like?
- What are our strategic goals?
- What are our anti-goals?
- What are the boundary conditions to stay within our strategy?
- How do we measure success?
- What is our strategic portfolio with options to achieve our goals?
- What new behavioral standards do we need to set?
- What do we need to strategically quit?
- What do we need to strategically sacrifice?
- How do we need to organize ourselves to drive execution?

7 The Executive Maverick: how to break industry norms to drive innovation

Here are 10 ideas to do things differently and drive innovation:

1. Create artificial scarcity: Booking.com always claims there are only a few rooms left.
2. Use the negative aspect of your product as an asset: The controversial taste of Red Bull signals sacrifice to improve performance.
3. Understand what is grudgingly accepted in your market by everyone else and change it: Robinhood introduced no-fee stock trading.
4. Break industry norms: IKEA lets customers build their own furniture.
5. Emulate the business values of your ideal client: John Deere works with independent dealers to support independent farmers.
6. Take out steps: Dell has removed brick-and-mortar stores.
7. Make it bigger: iPad Pro.
8. Make it smaller: iPad Mini.
9. Make it faster: Flash delivery for groceries.
10. Make it slower: Slow food.

8 Energy Shift: how to focus organizational energy to maximize value creation

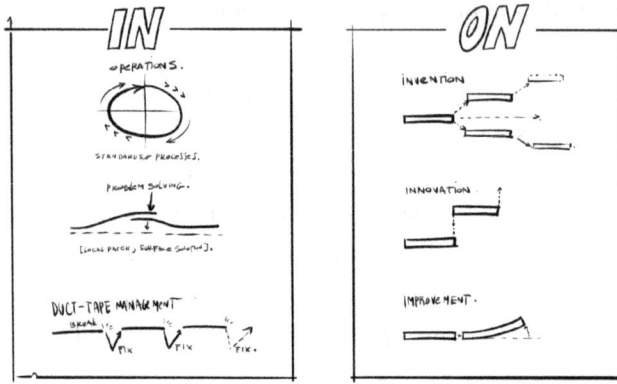

Figure 3.1 Energy Shift: the six areas where an organization spends its energy

How does your organization spend its energy?

Working in the business:

- Duct Tape Management: Issues are resolved, but they resurface repeatedly. Rinse and repeat. Think of a dysfunctional process that requires constant manual intervention.
- Problem-Solving: Issues are solved in a straightforward manner.
- Operations: These are all the activities necessary to run your current business.

Working on the business:

- Improvement: Activities that gradually create a better version of a process or system, such as company-wide Six Sigma initiatives or automation.
- Innovation: Introducing new approaches from outside the organization to create additional value.
- Invention: Developing completely new services or products that open new markets and attract new customers.

Ask yourself: How can I lead my organization to shift resources from working in the business to working on the business to accelerate value creation?

9 The Innovation Choice: how to focus on the right type of innovation

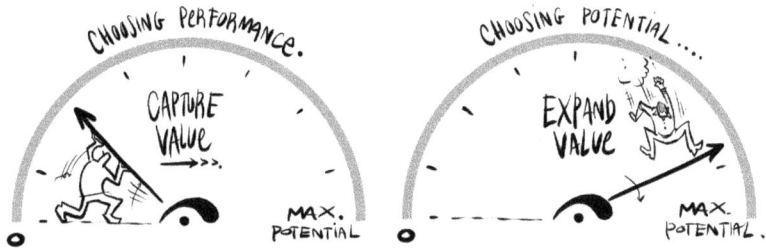

Figure 3.2 What to focus in order to create value

If your organization is overperforming versus its potential, focus on innovation to expand value.

If your organization is underperforming versus its potential, focus on innovation that improves capturing value.

10 The Ownership Ladder: how to drive ownership

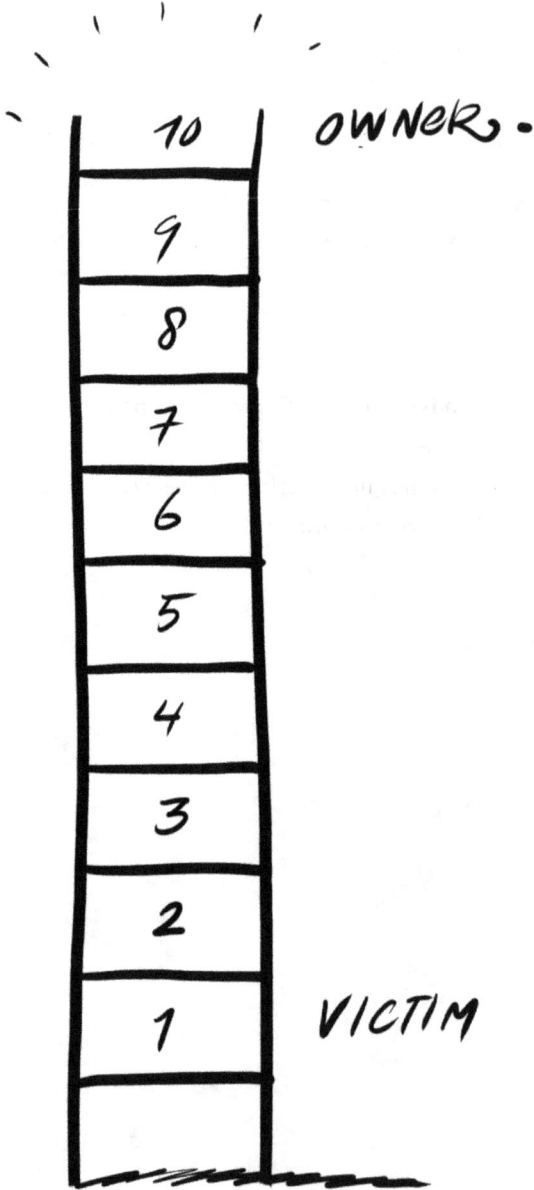

Figure 4.1 The Ownership Ladder

Where would you place your team on this ladder?

If you want to drive ownership, set new behavioral standards:

- Reduce Executive Babysitting. Avoid being:
  - The Referee
  - The Taskmaster
  - The Monkey Magnet
- More Playing to Win, less Playing Not to Lose
- More Agreements, less Expectations
- More Serving, less Pleasing
- More Curious, less Convinced
- More Principles, less Taste
- More Catalyst, less Kryptonite
  - "Yes, but ..."
  - Adding too much value
  - Listening to reply
  - Preemptive excuses
  - Negativity
  - Winner's obsession
  - Right at all costs
  - Unfiltered verbalization
  - Exaggerated language
  - Passive-aggressive attitude

11 The Smart Decision Grid: how to make better and faster decisions

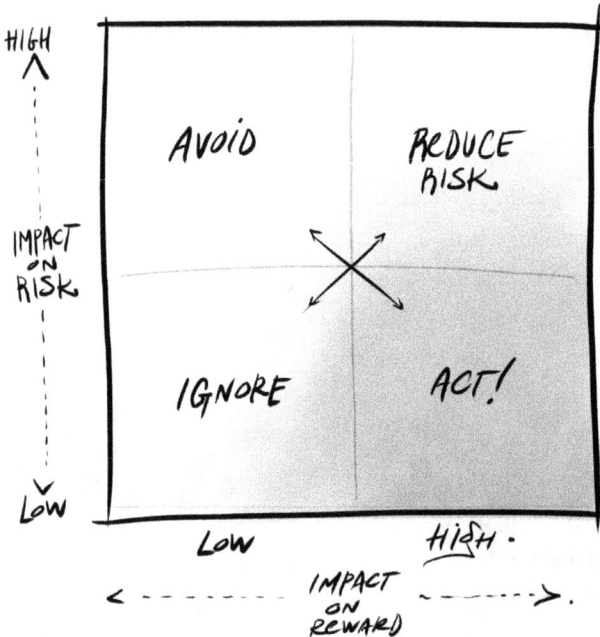

Figure 5.1 Smart Decision Grid: how to make better decisions using Risk versus Reward

Our decision-making energy is a limited resource and this matrix helps us to make optimal use of it. Thus, we get the following:

If the decision exposes you to low risk and a low reward, don't spend any mental energy on this decision. Make the decision by coin flip and move forward.

If the decision involves high risk and a low reward, avoid it at all costs.

If the decision exposes you to high risk and high reward, focus your mental energy on reducing risk. There are four ways to mitigate the downside of risk:

- Transfer risk
- Reduce risk
- Eliminate risk completely.
- Spread the risk

If the decision results in a low-risk, high-reward situation, move quickly with everything you have.

12 The Decision Catalyst: how to make better team decisions when information is scarce

If you want to create a culture that fosters better team decisions when information is scarce rather than limited, the key is to take action anyway. These distinctions will help:

- Speed versus rigor: If a team quickly reaches consensus on a difficult decision, it means they haven't given it enough thought. Reconvene, pursue different perspectives, and discuss the decision again later.
- Final versus flexible: A team decision is final unless new information arises that is relevant to the decision.
- Test versus commitment: A huge commitment, such as building a new factory, requires much more analysis than agreeing to conduct a small test. It's very difficult to change course after a significant commitment. A small test, however, allows you the opportunity to reverse course if needed.
- Reversible versus irreversible: Irreversible means you can't undo the decision—like trying to put toothpaste back into the tube. On the other hand, reversible decisions can be made quickly.
- Options versus constraints: Favor decisions that increase optionality and reduce constraints.

13 Strategic Quitting: how to do more of your highest and best use of time

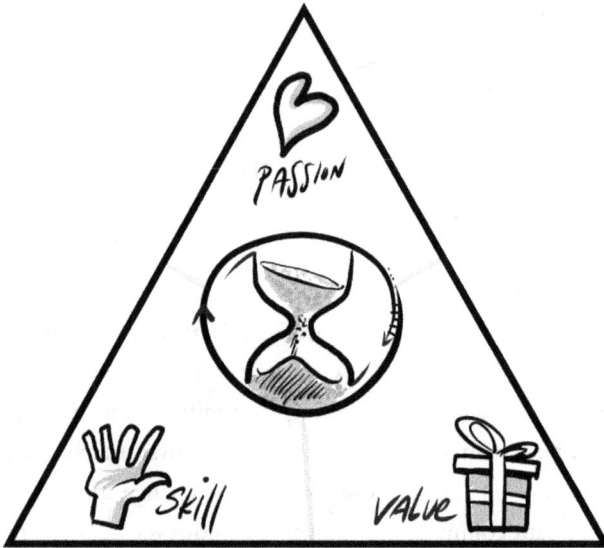

Figure 6.1 The Golden Triangle: how to determine the highest and best use of time

Your highest and best use of time are all activities which involve skill, passion and value creation for others.

Once you have determined your highest and best use of time, focus on strategic quitting. There are five ways you can begin to apply strategic quitting.

1. Elimination: The worst use of your time is not doing things inefficiently but doing things that shouldn't be done in the first place— in other words, becoming excellent at something irrelevant.
2. Delegation: Delegation means giving something that feels like work for you to someone for whom it feels like play.
3. Outsourcing: Either to a third party, or a system.
4. Optimization: What can you do to achieve the result in the laziest way possible?
5. Postponing: Put a project or initiative on hold.

14 Strategic Sacrifice: how to do more of your future highest and best use of time

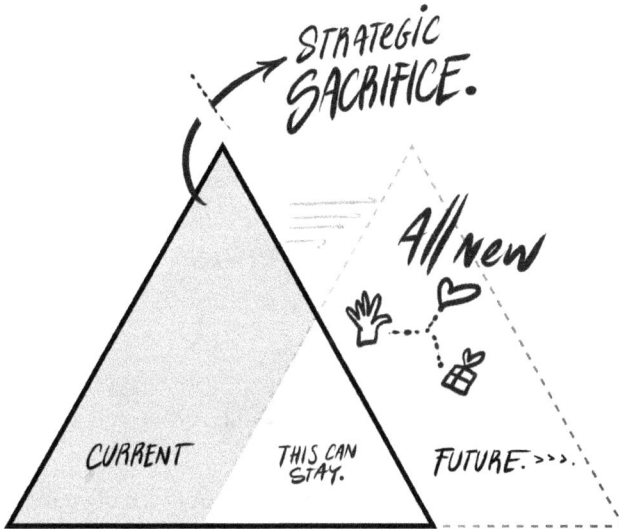

Figure 6.2 Strategic Sacrifice: how to shift value creation in time

Your current Golden Triangle may not be your future Golden Triangle. To identify your future Golden Triangle, ask yourself:

- Which new skills do I need to develop for my future, 3 years from now?
- What experiments do I need to conduct to identify the next level of my passion?
- What significant value can I create for my future clients with my new skillsets and passion?

15 Zero-Based Thinking: how to help your team to focus on the highest and best use of time

A fun way to engage your team in zero-based thinking is an exercise called "Lights On, Now What?" In this exercise, you pretend that you and your management team have just bought the company. It's your first day. You don't have any obligations, only big dreams and wild ambitions. How would you set up the organization from scratch?

Use zero-based thinking: *Knowing what I know now, which of the activities I'm currently engaged in would I choose not to even start if I could do it all over again?*

Typical areas to consider are:

- Processes and systems, such as HR onboarding and talent management.
- Clients, especially toxic clients who drain much of your energy and don't add much value anyway.
- Vendors who don't stick to agreements, are difficult, and require much hand-holding.
- Team members who decrease the energy level of others and require a lot of cleaning up after.
- Projects that are stuck and won't deliver the envisioned result.
- Products and services that are loss leaders and don't have a bright future.
- Markets that don't show any promise or growth.
- Technology that's not working.
- Add-ons to products and services that are not even currently valued by your clients.
- Data collection that is not turned into actionable insights.

16 High-Impact Meetings: how to build a high-performance meeting culture

Are your meetings the best meetings in the entire organization? The following principles are essential.

Meeting Objectives

A productive meeting can only have three objectives:

- **To make a decision.**
- **To brainstorm ideas.**
- **To drive project progress.**

Meeting Outcomes

The takeaway of any meeting consists of three parts:

- **Action list.** This contains all agreed-upon actions, the owner responsible for each action, and a date for completion. Only meeting participants can become the owner of an action.
- **Decision list.** This list records all decisions made during the meeting. It ensures clarity and prevents repeated discussions
- **Communication list.** This list ensures that individuals who were not in attendance are kept informed.

Meeting Choreography

Create a great performance with these three meeting rules:

- **No preparation, no seat on the table**.
- **No agenda, no meeting**.
- **Break Parkinson's Law**. Parkinson's Law states that a task will take as long as the time allocated to it.

Where are the biggest opportunity for improvement?

17 The Execution Machine: how to build a personal execution engine

The tangible part of your execution engine contains the following lists:

- Goal list.
- Project list.
- Action list.
- Someday/Maybe list.
- Waiting-for list.

The nontangible part of your execution engine contains the high-performance habits that fuel your productivity.

- Your inbox is not your action list.
- The 2-minute rule.
- Use Your Golden Hour.
- Apply Task-to-Time.
- Use the Swiss Cheese Technique.
- Apply the Productivity Trident.
- Eat Your Frog.
- Avoid the Bike Shed Fallacy
- Create Controlled Access.
  - Get rid of the "Open Door Policy."
  - Define Emergency Communication Protocols.
  - Be precise and accountable about any time agreements.

18 Ready for Anything: how to improve organizational resilience

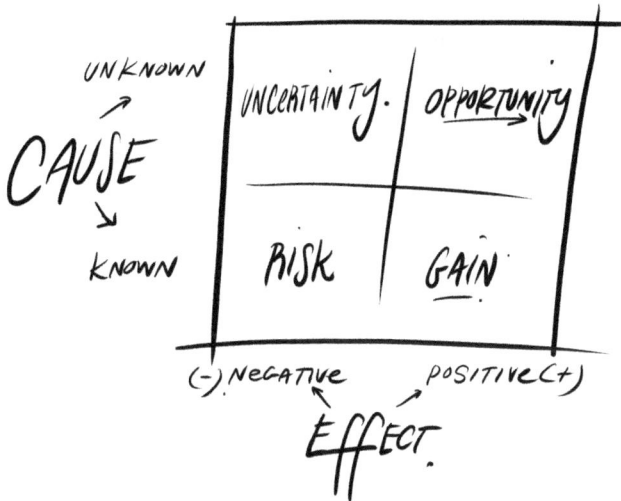

Figure 9.1 The Outcome Oracle: how to improve organizational resilience

This figure describes the impact of events on an organization. It plots cause, known versus unknown; and effect, negative versus positive.

The four quadrants:

- Uncertainty: If the cause is unknown and its effect is negative, we are dealing with uncertainty
- Opportunity: If the cause is unknown and its effect is positive, we are dealing with opportunity
- Risk: If the cause is known and its effect is negative, we are dealing with risk
- Gain: If the cause is known and its effect is positive, we are dealing with gain.

Resilience hinges on more exposure to positive effects and less exposure to negative effects, regardless of the cause.

This means that we can use three approaches to make our organization more resilient:

1. Create additional options to increase exposure to positive effects.
2. Reduce the factors that reduce optionality and make the organization less resilient.
3. Reduce the factors that amplify the negative effects of events.

19 The Genius Code: how to spot Supertalents

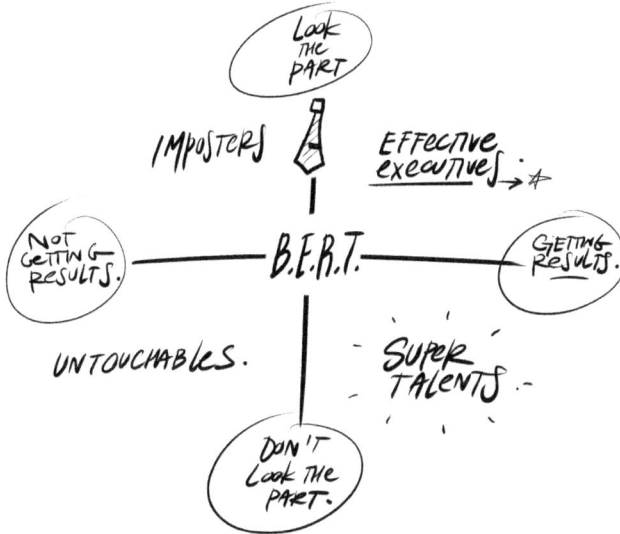

Figure 9.2 The Blunt Executive Review Tool: how to spot Supertalents

This tool reviews leaders on two dimensions:

The first dimension is getting results: How much they contribute to the strategic goals of the company.

The second dimension is looking the part: The appearance, mannerisms, habits, language, and behaviors you expect from your leaders.

The four categories in our BERT are:

1. The Untouchables: These leaders don't achieve results and don't look the part.
2. The Imposters: These leaders look the part but don't get results.
3. The Effective Executives: These leaders get results and look the part.
4. The Supertalents: These leaders get results but don't look the part. They are … different.

In turbulent times, the focus of any organization should be to spot and nurture its Supertalents.

20 The Premortem: how to increase the probability of strategy success

A premortem is the opposite of a postmortem. In a postmortem, mistakes are identified after a project has failed. In a premortem you creatively identify the likely major causes of failure before the project begins by imagining that the project has already failed. This exercise allows you to anticipate roadblocks in advance (thus cheating sudden project death) and significantly increases the success probability of your endeavor.

Here's how a premortem team exercise works:

- Imagine 5 years into the future. Your project has failed so miserably that the Harvard Business Review has asked to interview you about the reasons behind your failure.
- Divide the project team into small subgroups and have each group discuss what would be said in this interview.
- Gather the insights from all subgroups. The combined feedback will provide a clear picture of the main internal project risks.
- Mitigate risks by incorporating these insights into the project design from the very start: Which systems and processes do you need to build to avoid failure?

21 The Valley of Death: how to activate teams

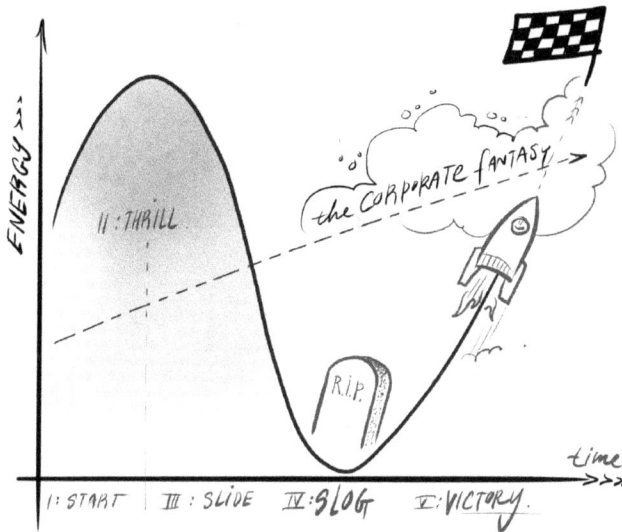

Figure 8.1 The Valley of Death: why strategies fail

The Valley of Death typically occurs at a point between the energy and excitement of setting a strategy or goal, and achieving that strategy or goal in the real world. The journey has five phases.

> **Phase I: The Start**: At first, your excitement is high. The vision is appealing, and you can't wait to get started.
>
> **Phase II: The Thrill**: You share the vision with others. They get excited too! Energy levels continue to rise. If energy dips this early in the project, this is a red flag that you need to find a more inspiring and optimistic team.
>
> **Phase III: The Slide:** You start the work. Progress is slow, obstacles are big, and energy is gradually draining.
>
> **Phase IV: The Slog:** Every day requires enormous effort to make a small amount of progress. It feels like wading through a dense swamp while wearing clown shoes. This is where dreams and projects die.

Phase V: The Victory: If you make it through the Slog, success becomes inevitable. You have passed through the Valley of Death, and energy skyrockets. You're exuberant—you made it.

Ask yourself:

- Where is my team right now?
- What do they need to prepare for the next phase?

22 High-Performance Teams: the nine focus areas to help your team overcome the Valley of Death

1. **Shared and ambitious goals:** At the start of a team meeting, ask team members to take out a blank sheet of paper and write down, in 30 seconds, the most important goals of the team for the year.

2. **Skin in the Game:** In an organization with full commitment, every team member has skin in the game. They speak with one voice and no one gets a pass.

3. **Helping each other improve:** The greatest opportunity for improvement lies in engaging in feedforward—focusing on how things can be done better in the future.

4. **Celebrate success:** Celebrating success for a leader involves actively looking for opportunities to genuinely acknowledge both individual and team contributions.

5. **Anticipate mistakes and blunders:** If you want to inspire your team to test new ideas, start a frank conversation about the mistakes you expect them to make and the blunders you expect them to avoid. Then give them the freedom to test many ideas, make many mistakes, and create real impact.

6. **Clear decision making:** The most important step in decision making for a leader is to decide at what level a decision should be made and then communicate this transparently to the team.

7. **Ask and give help.**

8. **Drive innovation:** If you want to build a culture of innovation, encourage your teams to:
   - Tinker and test more.
   - View surprises not as setbacks but as opportunities.
   - Always be curious, not convinced.

9. **Use Supertalents:** If you want to identify your personal supertalent, or the supertalents of your team members, look for three signs:

   1. You rely on your supertalent whenever you face a complex problem or an exciting opportunity.

   2. People frequently come to you for help in the area of your supertalent.

   3. You love to immerse yourself in new perspectives related to your supertalent. The books you read and the websites you visit likely revolve around it.

23 Raising the Bar: how to help others improve

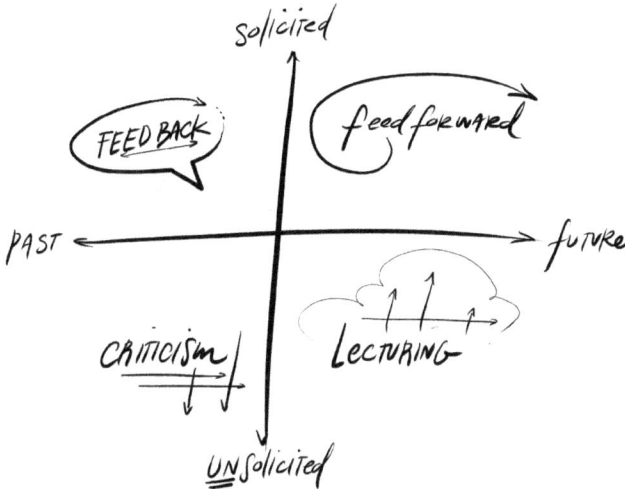

Figure 8.2 How to help others improve

This framework tells a clear story. Unsolicited advice is often perceived as criticism or lecturing, which is ineffective. As a leader, ensure that your ideas come in response to an explicit request.

When it's about observed behavior, this is feedback. The greatest opportunity for improvement lies in engaging in feedforward—focusing on how things can be done better in the future.

The next time you want improvement in an area, such as time management, ask a few trusted friends or colleagues for their best ideas. Then, pick one or two and start implementing them. A team culture of solicited feedback and the use of the feedforward approach reduces resistance, builds trust, and increases performance. As a leader, set the expectation that every team member is committed to helping others improve

24 The Decision-Making Ziggurat: how to balance leadership control and team commitment in decision making

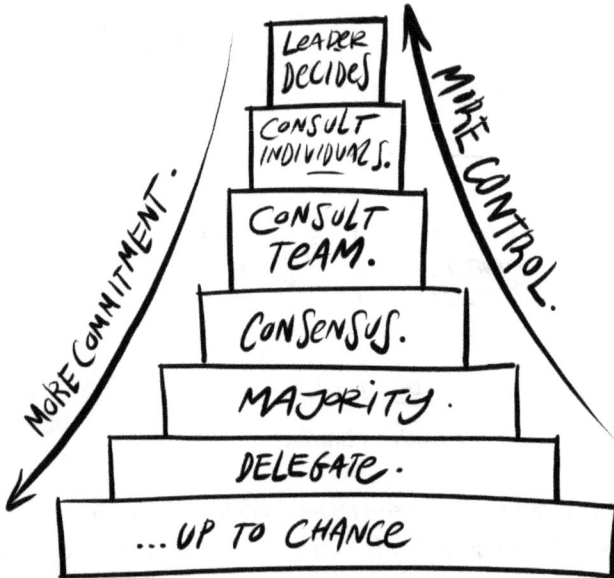

Figure 8.3 The Decision-Making Ziggurat: how to balance control and commitment in decision making

Starting at the top of the Ziggurat:

- First level: The leader decides. This typically happens with critical decisions, such as firing a management team member.
- Second level: The leader consults individual team members, who provide input, after which the leader decides.
- Third level: The leader consults the entire team, then makes a final decision.
- Fourth level: The decision is made by team consensus. Every team member can live with the outcome, though it may not be ideal for everyone.
- Fifth level: The decision is made by majority vote. If the leader is in the minority, she has given up control over the decision.

- Sixth level: The decision is delegated to a team member.
- Seventh level: The decision is delegated to chance (e.g., a coin flip).

The most important step in decision making for a leader is to decide at what level a decision should be made and then communicate this transparently to the team.

25 The Legacy Pyramid: how to elevate leadership focus

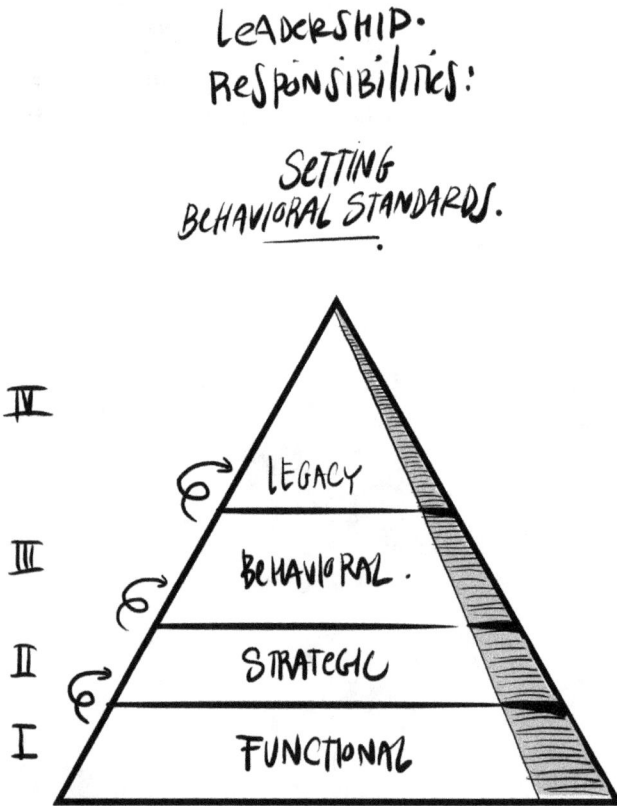

LeADeRSHIP·
ReSPoNSIBiliTies:

SeTTiNG
BeHAVIORAL STANDARDS.

IV

III   LEGACY

II   BEHAVIORAL.

II   STRATEGIC

I   FUNCTIONAL

Figure 10.1 The Legacy Pyramid: how to elevate leadership focus

This figure describes the hierarchy of responsibility of the leaders in your organization.

Starting at the top:

- Level 1: Legacy Responsibility. Leadership is defined as making yourself obsolete.
- Level 2: Behavioral Responsibility. Leaders define shared standards and extensively role-model them throughout the organization, regularly crossing functions and silos.
- Level 3: Strategic Responsibility. In this case, the focus is on achieving the overall strategy of the organization. Typically,

functional goals are sacrificed to achieve the overall goals of the organization.

- Level 4: Functional Responsibility. The main objective is to ensure that a function in the organization, such as HR, finance, or IT, runs smoothly. Success is determined by achieving the goals of the function itself.

You can't solve a structural issue at the level where the effect of the issue consistently occurs. You need to go a level up.

About the Author

Paul Rulkens is a global authority on high-performance leadership, strategy, and exponential growth. With a sharp focus on simplifying complexity and amplifying results, Paul has helped senior executives and organizations around the world achieve extraordinary outcomes by doing less. His signature frameworks, including *The Michelangelo Principle*, challenge conventional thinking and empower leaders to remove the unnecessary and focus on what truly matters.

Paul's work has attracted a prestigious list of global clients, including McKinsey & Company, Siemens, UBER, Johnson & Johnson, ASML, and Nestlé. Across industries, Paul has helped these organizations streamline decision making, activate high-performance teams, and create systems that thrive under pressure. His clients consistently report measurable results, including improved profitability, operational efficiency, and leadership transformation.

A thought leader and engaging speaker, Paul's TED talk, *Why the Majority Is Always Wrong*, has been viewed over 6 million times. Known for his ability to distill complex ideas into actionable insights, Paul delivers over 30 keynotes annually to leaders and organizations across the globe.

In addition, Paul is a senior fellow at the Conference Board, where he contributes to advancing leadership insights and best practices for global executives.

At the core of Paul's philosophy is a simple yet profound belief: Greatness is achieved not by adding more, but by removing the unnecessary. Like Michelangelo chiseling away the "non-David," Paul helps leaders carve out clarity, focus, and impact. His strategies are practical, innovative, and designed to deliver immediate results.

Paul's mission goes beyond short-term wins. Inspired by the principles in *The Michelangelo Principle*, he helps leaders create lasting legacies by building resilient systems that persist long after they are gone. His multidisciplinary approach—drawing from fields like physics, history, and engineering—brings fresh perspectives that resonate with leaders navigating today's fast-paced business landscape.

If you're ready to simplify leadership, unlock exponential growth, and leave a legacy of sustainable success, Paul Rulkens is your trusted partner. Whether through an inspiring keynote or a tailored consulting engagement, Paul delivers the tools, clarity, and vision to help you achieve extraordinary results.

Visit www.paulrulkens.com to learn more and discover how Paul can help you and your organization succeed.

Recommended Readings

Allen, David. *Getting Things Done: The Art of Stress-Free Productivity*. Penguin Books, 2015.

Djukich, Dusan. *Straight-Line Leadership*. Robert D. Reed Publishers, 2011.

Godin, Seth. *The Dip*. Piatkus Books, 2007.

Goldsmith, Marshall. *What Got You Here Won't Get You There*. Hyperion, 2007.

Kahneman, Daniel. *Thinking, Fast and Slow*. Penguin Publishing, 2011.

Kepner, Charles H., and Benjamin B. Tregoe. *The New Rational Manager: An Updated Edition for a New World*. Princeton Research Press, 1997.

Koch, Richard. *The Power Laws*. Nicholas Brealey Publishing, 2000.

Rulkens, Paul. *The Power of Preeminence*. Vakmedianet, 2017.

Rulkens, Paul. *How Successful Engineers Become Great Business Leaders*. Business Expert Press, 2018.

Taleb, Nassim Nicholas. *Antifragile: Things That Gain from Disorder*. Random House, 2012.

Tracy, Brian. *Goals!* Berrett-Koehler Publishers, 2004.

Weiss, Alan. *Million Dollar Consulting*. McGraw-Hill, 2003.

Index